Social Science

Social and Political Life – II

Textbook for Class VII

Social Science

Social and Political Life – II

Textbook for Class VII

राष्ट्रीय शैक्षिक अनुसंधान और प्रशिक्षण परिषद्
NATIONAL COUNCIL OF EDUCATIONAL RESEARCH AND TRAINING

First Edition
February 2007 Phalguna 1928
Reprinted
February 2008 Magha 1929
March 2009 Phalguna 1930
January 2010 Magha 1931
December 2010 Agrahayana 1932
January 2012 Magha 1933
November 2012 Kartika 1934
November 2013 Kartika 1935
December 2014 Pausa 1936
January 2016 Pausa 1937

PD 460T RSP

₹50.00

Printed on 80 GSM paper with NCERT watermark

Published at the Publication Division by the Secretary, National Council of Educational Research and Training, Sri Aurobindo Marg, New Delhi 110 016 and printed at Swan Press, B-71, Naraina Industrial Area, Phase-II, New Delhi - 28

ISBN 81-7450-672-1

OFFICES OF THE PUBLICATION DIVISION, NCERT

NCERT Campus
Sri Aurobindo Marg
New Delhi 110 016 **Phone : 011-26562708**

108, 100 Feet Road
Hosdakere Halli Extension
Banashankari III Stage
Bangaluru 560 085 **Phone : 080-26725740**

Navjivan Trust Building
P.O.Navjivan
Ahmedabad 380 014 **Phone : 079-27541446**

CWC Campus
Opp. Dhankal Bus Stop
Panihati
Kolkata 700 114 **Phone : 033-25530454**

CWC Complex
Maligaon
Guwahati 781 021 **Phone : 0361-2674869**

Publication Team

Head, Publication Division	:	*Dinesh Kumar*
Chief Editor	:	*Shveta Uppal*
Chief Business Manager	:	*Gautam Ganguly*
Chief Production Officer (Incharge)	:	*Arun Chitkara*
Assistant Editor	:	*Shashi Chadha*
Production Assistant	:	*Mukesh Gaur*

Cover, Layout
Orijit Sen with Splash! Communications

Illustrations
Orijit Sen

Foreword

The National Curriculum Framework (NCF), 2005, recommends that children's life at school must be linked to their life outside the school. This principle marks a departure from the legacy of bookish learning which continues to shape our system and causes a gap between the school, home and community. The syllabi and textbooks developed on the basis of NCF signify an attempt to implement this basic idea. They also attempt to discourage rote learning and the maintenance of sharp boundaries between different subject areas. We hope these measures will take us significantly further in the direction of a child-centred system of education outlined in the National Policy on Education (1986).

The success of this effort depends on the steps that school principals and teachers will take to encourage children to reflect on their own learning and to pursue imaginative activities and questions. We must recognise that given space, time and freedom, children generate new knowledge by engaging with the information passed on to them by adults. Treating the prescribed textbook as the sole basis of examination is one of the key reasons why other resources and sites of learning are ignored. Inculcating creativity and initiative is possible if we perceive and treat children as participants in learning, not as receivers of a fixed body of knowledge.

These aims imply considerable change in school routines and mode of functioning. Flexibility in the daily timetable is as necessary as rigour in implementing the annual calendar so that the required number of teaching days is actually devoted to teaching. The methods used for teaching and evaluation will also determine how effective this textbook proves for making children's life at school a happy experience, rather than a source of stress or boredom. Syllabus designers have tried to address the problem of curricular burden by restructuring and reorienting knowledge at different stages with greater consideration for child psychology and the time available for teaching. The textbook attempts to enhance this endeavour by giving higher priority and space to opportunities for contemplation and wondering, discussion in small groups, and activities requiring hands-on experience.

The National Council of Educational Research and Training (NCERT) appreciates the hard work done by the textbook development committee responsible for this book. We wish to thank the Chairperson of the advisory group in Social Sciences, Professor Hari Vasudevan, the Chief Advisor, Sarada Balagopalan and the Advisor, Arvind Sardana for guiding the work of this committee. Several teachers contributed to the development of this textbook; we are grateful to their principals for making this possible. We are indebted to the institutions and organisations which have generously permitted us to draw upon their resources, material and personnel. We are especially grateful to the members of the National Monitoring Committee, appointed by the Department of Secondary and Higher Education, Ministry of Human Resources Development under the Chairpersonship of Professor Mrinal Miri and Professor G.P. Deshpande, for their valuable time and contribution. As an organisation committed to systemic reform and continuous improvement in the quality of its products, NCERT welcomes comments and suggestions which will enable us to undertake further revision and refinement.

Director

New Delhi — National Council of Educational Research and Training

20 November 2006

Textbook Development Committee

Chairperson, Advisory Committee for Social Science Textbooks at the Upper Primary Level

Hari Vasudevan, *Professor*, Department of History, University of Calcutta, Kolkata

Chief Advisor

Sarada Balagopalan, Centre for the Study of Developing Societies (CSDS), Rajpur Road, Delhi

Advisor

Arvind Sardana, Eklavya – Institute for Educational Research and Innovative Action, Madhya Pradesh

Members

Anjali Monteiro, *Professor*, Tata Institute of Social Sciences (TISS), Mumbai

Anjali Noronha, Eklavya – Institute for Educational Research and Innovative Action, Madhya Pradesh

Anuradha Sen, H-701, Som Vihar, R.K. Puram, New Delhi

Dipta Bhog, Nirantar – Centre for Gender and Education, New Delhi

Krishna Menon, *Reader*, Lady Shri Ram College, New Delhi

Latika Gupta, *Consultant*, Department of Elementary Education (DEE), NCERT

M.V. Srinivasan, *Lecturer*, Department of Education in Social Sciences and Humanities (DESSH), NCERT

Malini Ghose, Nirantar – Centre for Gender and Education, New Delhi

Mary E. John, *Director*, Centre for Women's Development Studies (CWDS), New Delhi

N.B. Sarojini, Sama – Resource Group for Women and Health, New Delhi

Rangan Chakravarty, A 4/7, Golf Green Urban Complex, Phase 1, Kolkata

Sanjay Dubey, *Reader*, DESSH, NCERT

Shobha Bajpai, Government Middle School, Uda, District Harda, Madhya Pradesh

Sukanya Bose, Eklavya *Research Fellow*, 66 F Sector 8, Jasola Vihar, New Delhi

Member-coordinator

Malla V.S.V. Prasad, *Lecturer*, DESSH, NCERT

Acknowledgements

This book has benefited from its association with several individuals and institutions. These include Poonam Batra, Piu Dutt, S. Mohinder and Aditya Nigam who read most of the chapters in the book and gave us helpful feedback. In addition, Rajeev Bhargav, Kaushik Ghosh, Anu Gupta, Sunil and A.V. Ramani discussed ideas and commented on particular chapters. V.Geetha was gracious in agreeing to read all of the chapters and her extensive comments have enriched this book substantially. Anjali Monteiro and S. Shankar shared with us their ideas on the media at different stages and helped us expand upon that particular chapter in meaningful ways.

Tultul Biswas helped us in finding an appropriate poem for our last chapter and Vinay Mahajan was gracious in allowing us to use this. Sanchira Biswas and Dipta Bhog translated this poem into English while Ravikant assisted in finalising this translation. Smriti Vohra also agreed to do some last minute editing without realising how much she had taken on, and we thank her for her time and careful editing. Similar to his role in the Class VI book, Alex George has been of significant help with his insights, ideas and information. Urvashi Butalia continues to be generous with her time and willingness to serve as editor, thereby ensuring that this text has gained from her perceptive reading.

We thank Zubaan for allowing us to use poster images from their book *Poster Women: A Visual History of the Women's Movement in India*. We would also like to thank Trimurti Films Private Ltd. for allowing the use of the *Deewar* clip. Partners For Law and Development graciously allowed us to use their image on page 63. The Principal, teachers and students of Class VI B at the Kendriya Vidyalaya II at Hindon, Ghaziabad readily agreed to work on the wallpaper and the collage that we have used in the book and were kind in allowing us to photograph this as well. We would also like to thank Yogender S Rajput, PRO, Northern Railway, and National Centre for Promotion of Employment for Disabled People (NCPEDP) for the public advertisements. M. Quraishy at SARAI also extended his help when required and we thank him for this.

The photographs that this book uses were procured from various sources and we are deeply grateful to all these institutions and individuals. The Centre for Science and Environment (CSE) was more than generous with their photographs and Amit Shankar and Anil with their time. *Outlook Magazine* also shared with us, at very short notice, photos from their archives. Sheeba Chacchi provided us with her photos for the photo-essay on the women's movement. Salil Chaturvedi and Shahid Datawala helped provide appropriate images from their collection. Mahesh Basadia provided us with photos of the Tawa Matsya Sangh (TMS) and the Mahila Balvikas Department at Dewas gave us the image of the *Anganwadi*. Harsh Man Rai and Baji Rao Pawar also contributed their photos as well as helped click new photos that we needed. M.V. Srinivasan helped with coordinating the photos from Erode. Devajyoti Dutta created the advertisements used in the advertising chapter. We thank Navdanya for some of the images used for the collage on health. Sarada Balagopalan also helped click some of the images used in this book.

The passion and patience that Orijit Sen and Salil Chaturvedi have invested as the main illustrator and designer of this book can be seen in every page, and we thank them for this.

Eklavya played a crucial role in the translation of this book into Hindi and we would, in particular, like to thank Rashmi Paliwal for her supervision of the process and Tultul Biswas for helping facilitate this.

Several institutions have played a key role in not only being understanding about our pre-occupation with this book but in actively assisting its development in numerous ways. The Centre for the Study of Developing Societies (CSDS), Eklavya, Nirantar, Centre for Women's Development Studies (CWDS) and Sama have been generous in their support.

Introductory note for teachers

There is a substantial difference between Civics and Social and Political Life, not only in terms of the topics covered but also in the pedagogic approaches required in each subject area. Keeping these in mind, this Introduction attempts to clarify certain aspects of Social and Political Life.

What is Social and Political Life?

Social and Political Life (SPL) is a new subject area in middle school social science that has replaced the earlier subject of Civics. The National Curriculum Framework (NCF) 2005 strongly argues that Civics should be discontinued and its focus on government institutions and functioning should be tempered in the new subject that replaces it. SPL, as its name suggests, focuses on topics related to social, political and economic life in contemporary India.

What pedagogical approach does SPL use?

SPL's use of 'real-life' situations is a marked departure from Civics. SPL uses these real situations to teach concepts because it recognises that children learn best through concrete experiences. It uses material that draws upon the experiential understanding of familial and social issues that middle school children bring to the classroom. SPL further develops the learner's abilities to critically understand and analyse these issues in keeping with the tenets of the Indian Constitution.

This pedagogical approach tends to avoid the use of definitions to sum up a concept. Instead, it uses case studies and narratives to explain concepts. The concepts embedded within the narratives are made clear through the in-text and end-text questions. The aim is to have the learner understand the concept through their own experiences and write about it in their own words.

This often means that there is seldom one 'correct' answer to the questions posed. However there is a wrong answer. Teachers should try to gauge whether an answer to a question adequately reflects the learner's understanding of the concept being discussed.

Case studies and narratives used in SPL are a mix of rural and urban examples.

Given that children learn best through understanding and applying concepts to local realities, can a 'national' textbook adequately reflect the many 'locals' that make up the nation?

SPL functions by the pedagogic principle that children learn best through an experiential understanding of concepts. This poses a contradiction when the effort is to write a 'national' textbook, because a national text can neither sufficiently represent all the various aspects of the various locals, nor fix the sociocultural background of the child for whom the book is intended. Therefore, the case studies and narratives used in SPL are a mix of rural and urban examples in which the assumed learner is not easily discernible.

The SPL text specifically names communities, for example, Dalit, Muslim, poor, etc. SPL counts on the teacher to transact the material with a firm committment to respecting the dignity of all students.

In addition to the important job of transacting the text, what crucial role does SPL expect teachers to play in the classroom?

SPL counts on the teacher to play a very significant role in the classroom for the following reasons. First, the SPL text specifically names communities (for example: Dalit, Muslim, poor etc.) in its discussion of various issues and this may lead to some discomfort in a classroom that has a student population from different sociocultural and (perhaps) economic backgrounds. We expect the teacher to play a crucial role in transacting this material with a sensitivity and firm commitment to respecting the dignity of all students in the classroom and the school. Second, given the limited ability of this 'national' text to engage the local we also envision the teacher playing a major role in adding local examples to the discussion of concepts, provided these remain true to the logic and understanding of each concept as intended by the book's authors.

How does the SPL help the learner assimilate the values enshrined in the Constitution?

At first glance it might appear to some that unlike Civics, SPL's focus on 'real' examples contradicts the tenets of the Constitution. Such a focus, however, is a technique utilised in SPL in response to a critique of Civics textbooks that always only discussed the ideal and seldom deliberated upon the reality that was very different. Since the learner is already aware of such realities, to avoid discussing them would make the learning of social and political concepts didactic and disconnected. Instead, SPL uses this embedded awareness to make the learner understand and accept not only the legitimacy but also the urgency of the values enshrined in the Constitution. Additionally, this approach allows the learner to understand the role of people's struggles in the realisation of these values.

What are the issues included in the Class VII textbook?

The theme for the Class VII book is the crucial role that equality plays in Indian democracy. This theme also serves as one of the Units in addition to which the book has four more Units. These include Health and State Government; Gender; Media and Advertising; and Markets. Each Unit consists of two consecutive chapters, except in the case of the first Unit in which they make up the first and the concluding chapters of the text.

What elements does the Class VII book utilise to explain selected issues?

◆ **Storyboards:** One component of the feedback regarding Class VI book (Social and Political Life-I) was that teachers needed more assistance in understanding where fictional narratives began and ended and in identifying the central concepts within these. With this in mind, this year's book

Yes. I think this promotes a new way of expressing love and care. I would like to try this new brand.
Thank you Madam!
SALE

introduces storyboards to clearly indicate which segments have been fictionalised, and to draw the learner into the narrative through the use of visuals that are often more expressive than lines of text. Specific concepts raised through the storyboards are analysed in the accompanying text.

◆ **Unit Pages:** Each Unit begins with a Unit Page for teachers to help highlight the main points raised in the two chapters.

◆ **Note on Evaluation:** As with the Class VI text, this book does not contain definitions or a synthesis of concepts. While we recognise that this makes it difficult for teachers to evaluate what the child has learnt, our attempt is also to try and shift some of the understanding amongst teachers on what children are expected to learn and how such learning should be evaluated. This book contains a short note on evaluation procedures that we hope will assist teachers in their efforts to move students away from rote learning.

◆ **Glossary:** The inclusion of a Glossary with each chapter is intended to offer the learner greater clarity on the language used in the text. The words of the Glossary are NOT limited to concepts, and it should not be viewed as something to be memorised with the expectation that such rote learning will contribute to conceptual understanding.

◆ **In-text and End-text Questions:** As with the Class VI text, this year's book includes in-text and end-text questions, making use of visual material and experiential analysis. In-text questions found within the text can be used to assess the extent to which content has been assimilated. End-text questions usually cover the main concepts raised by the chapter and ask learners to explain these in their own words.

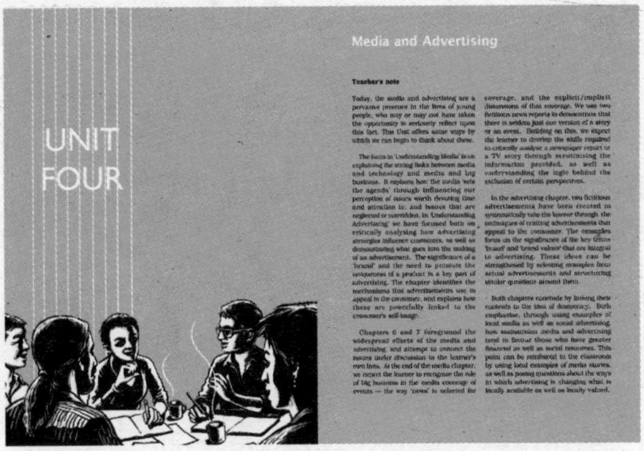

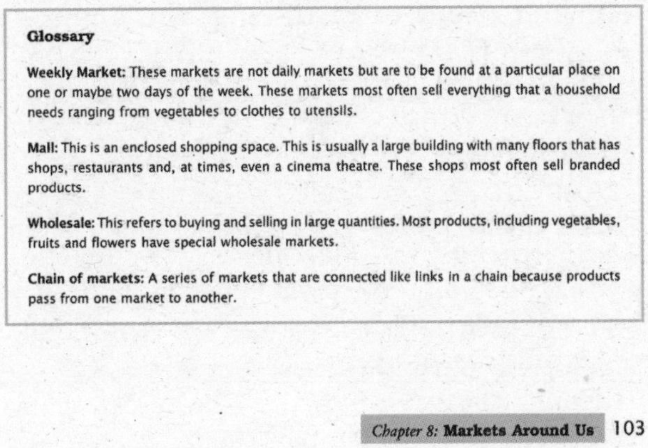
Glossary

Weekly Market: These markets are not daily markets but are to be found at a particular place on one or maybe two days of the week. These markets most often sell everything that a household needs ranging from vegetables to clothes to utensils.

Mall: This is an enclosed shopping space. This is usually a large building with many floors that has shops, restaurants and, at times, even a cinema theatre. These shops most often sell branded products.

Wholesale: This refers to buying and selling in large quantities. Most products, including vegetables, fruits and flowers have special wholesale markets.

Chain of markets: A series of markets that are connected like links in a chain because products pass from one market to another.

Chapter 8: **Markets Around Us** 103

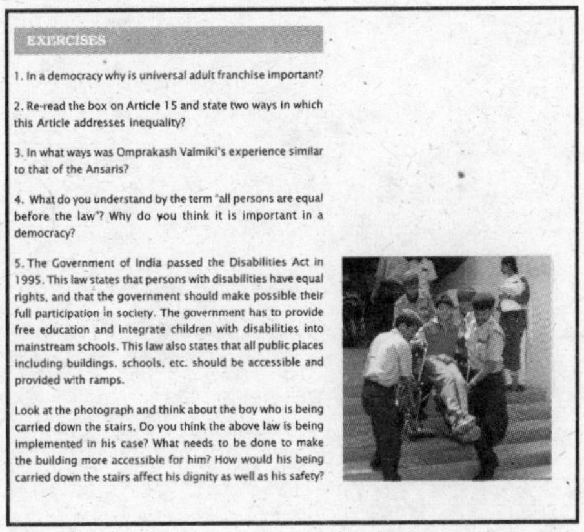
EXERCISES

1. In a democracy why is universal adult franchise important?

2. Re-read the box on Article 15 and state two ways in which this Article addresses inequality?

3. In what ways was Omprakash Valmiki's experience similar to that of the Ansaris?

4. What do you understand by the term "all persons are equal before the law"? Why do you think it is important in a democracy?

5. The Government of India passed the Disabilities Act in 1995. This law states that persons with disabilities have equal rights, and that the government should make possible their full participation in society. The government has to provide free education and integrate children with disabilities into mainstream schools. This law also states that all public places including buildings, schools, etc. should be accessible and provided with ramps.

Look at the photograph and think about the boy who is being carried down the stairs. Do you think the above law is being implemented in his case? What needs to be done to make the building more accessible for him? How would his being carried down the stairs affect his dignity as well as his safety?

Teacher's note on evaluation

Rethinking the ways in which we evaluate learning is a difficult task but one that this new subject area requires. Over the years our evaluation system has for the most part rewarded students who learnt by rote. This involuntarily encouraged many teachers to mark or underline the answers in the text and in this way a vicious cycle in which each reinforced the other, was produced. It is this system that needs to be changed to relieve both the teacher and the student. Teachers will play a significant role in changing evaluation and this note is an effort in this direction.

On questions

Teachers need to begin by insisting that evaluation be based on 'new' questions. These will be similar to the ones used in the text, but not the same. Students will be expected to answer these questions in their own words. The confidence to do this needs to be built in the students and language corrections should, therefore, be tactful and gentle.

Teachers will also need to design a variety of questions that cover a range of skills. Questions that demand recalling information by rote should be minimal. Instead, there needs to be different kinds of questions based on the main conceptual ideas of each chapter. Some may be designed to draw upon the learner's ability to reason; to compare and contrast experiences; and to infer and extrapolate from situations provided.

The following are some examples taken from this text to explain the above:

Ability to reason

These questions aim to gauge the extent to which the learner has understood the concepts included in the chapter and is able to articulate its main ideas in their own words as well as apply these to different contexts. Examples of this include:

What do you understand by the term, "all persons are equal before the law"? Why do you think it is important in a democracy?

Can you list two ways in which you feel that advertising effects issues of equality in a democracy?

Why should the decisions taken by the Chief Minister and other ministers be debated in the Legislative Assembly?

How do you think your neighbourhood shop gets its goods? Find out and explain with some examples.

Compare and contrast experiences

These questions require the learner to draw upon the main ideas in the text by comparing and contrasting concrete situations. These questions often involve the child's own experiences. Examples of this include:

What is the difference between the work that MLAs do in the Assembly and the work done by government departments?

In what ways do the experiences of Samoan children and teenagers differ from your own experiences of growing up? Is there anything described in this experience that you wish were part of your growing up?

Compare the earnings per shirt of the worker in the garment factory, the garment exporter and the shop-owner in the US. What do you find?

What differences do you find between private and public health services in your area? Use the following table to write about these.

Facility	Cost of services	Availability of service
Private		
Public		

Infer and extrapolate from situations

This type of question is important to SPL because of the extensive use of narratives to explain concepts as well as the constant reference to the learner's own experiences. It is these questions that link the narrative to the underlying concept. The learner's ability to understand the narrative as well as its explication of the concept can be gauged through these questions.

Why do you think Omprakash Valmiki was treated unequally by his teacher? Imagine yourself as Omprakash Valmiki and write four lines about how you would feel if you were in the above situation?

Were Harmeet and Shonali correct in saying that Harmeet's mother did not work?

In India it is often said that we are unable to provide health services for all because the government does not have enough money and facilities. After reading the left hand column above do you think that this is true? Discuss.

What does this ad want me to feel when I use this brand?

Interpreting visual material

Similarly students should have an opportunity to read and interpret visual material. Hence there should be questions based on pictures, tables, flowcharts, etc.

① Look at the photograph and think about the boy who is being carried down the stairs. Do you think the above law is being implemented in his case? What needs to be done to make the building more accessible for him? How would his being carried down the stairs affect his dignity as well as his safety?

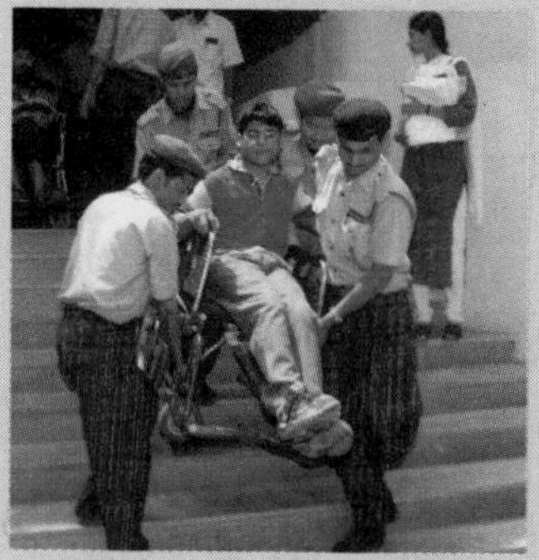

② Can you give this diagram a title? What do you understand about the link between media and big business from this diagram?

BIG BUSINESS HOUSES
Some own radio, TV, newspaper
advertise their products
People buy products seen in the media. Money, therefore, flows back to big business houses
MEDIA
promotes products through advertisements
READERS, VIEWERS, LISTENERS

③ The shirt below shows the profit made by the businessperson, and the various costs that he had to pay. Find out from the diagram below, what the cost price includes.

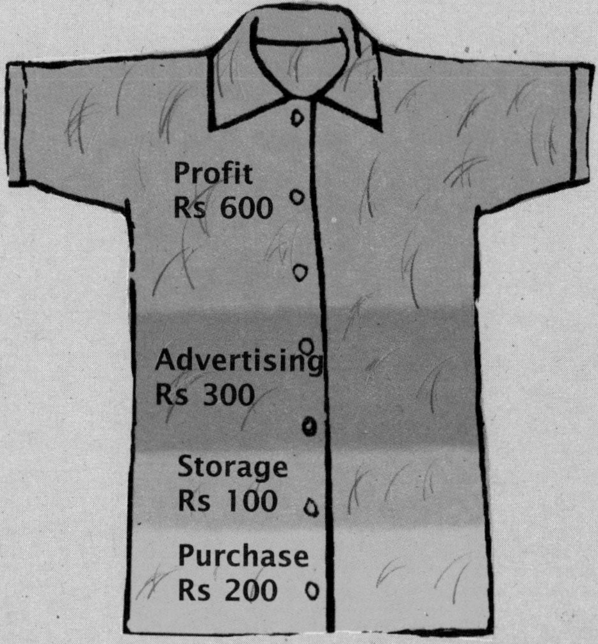

Profit Rs 600
Advertising Rs 300
Storage Rs 100
Purchase Rs 200

On answers

Since the learner is being asked to write in their own words teachers will need to stop expecting 'exact' responses. Instead, the learner should be encouraged to state in their own words their understanding of the material and concepts they've read. Their comprehension, ability to soundly reason and communicate their ideas is what needs to be evaluated.

It would also be fair to expect a range of correct answers when the learner is asked to think through a particular narrative situation and apply the underlying concept. It is crucial that teachers discuss a common evaluation scheme that helps them distinguish between the range of correct answers as well as more crucially identify wrong answers.

An example of what we mean by a range of responses to a question, as well as a wrong answer is provided below:

If you were one of the Ansaris how would you have responded to the property dealer's suggestion that you change your name?

Range of right answers

"If I were one of the Ansaris I would have decided not to change my name because this would deeply affect my dignity and self-respect."	This is a short, clear answer that indicates good comprehension and ability to communicate ideas.
"I would not change my name if I were one of the Ansaris because this is the name that my family has had for generations and it would make me feel bad to say that I was someone else."	Here, the learner does not use the word 'dignity', but has understood the concept and is attempting to communicate this in her own words.
"I will take up the property dealer's suggestion and change my name. I will do this because I am tired of looking for a flat. I would not like to do so but I need a place to stay."	On the face of it, this might appear to be the wrong answer since the learner agrees with the property dealer's suggestion. If a question has asked for an opinion it could be either way. As long as the learner puts forward a logical argument to support their opinion, the answer is right. This answer shows that they have understood the idea of the Ansaris' dignity being affected.

Wrong answer

"If I were one of the Ansaris I will agree to change my name because this will increase my dignity."	This question is asked as part of the section on 'Recognising Dignity' in the text. The learner has not been able to make the connection between the discrimination and disrespect faced by the Ansaris, and their loss of dignity.

Other forms of evaluation

We need to demystify the stress on examinations as the best tool for evaluating the learner. Rather than wait for alternate evaluation structures to trickle down from the higher grades, we need to use the learner's years in middle school to experiment with other ways of evaluation. For this purpose we need to use different methods, some of which are briefly discussed below –

◆ **Open-book exercises:** As the name implies 'open-book' is a process in which the learner is allowed to refer to the textbook while answering a question. Open book exercises offer children an opportunity to pick out answers without feeling the burden of "remembering the details". The learner would be asked to read portions of the text again with the question in mind. New questions are essential for this exercise. Questions based on the learner's ability to infer, extrapolate and apply concepts are ideal for open-book exercises. Answering the question in the learner's own words should be emphasised.

◆ **Oral reasoning and comprehension:** Children express so much through speaking and sharing in a classroom. Yet, most often, our current educational system tends to regard this as 'useless talk'. Learning from peers and expressing themselves through the spoken word is something that needs to be encouraged. Oral evaluation exercises provide an avenue through which to value this. A number of in-text questions in this book can be answered orally and the teacher should begin this process in the classroom.

◆ **Collective project work:** Collective project work is another way to evaluate students. Preparing a wall-paper is one such example used in the text. The expectations from these projects should be reasonable and limited to what learners can do on their own. Project work should be done in the classroom and not as homework. Many end-text questions in this book can be converted into small projects.

These forms of evaluation help emphasise that learning is continuous and happens in multiple ways. Evaluation should be designed to enable and encourage this learning and not be reduced to a filtering mechanism.

To share ideas and for any further clarification contact us at: spl_ncert@hotmail.com

Contents

UNIT ONE

Equality in Indian Democracy

Teacher's note

This Unit introduces the learner to the critical role of equality in democracy, with specific reference to India. The Constitution of India guarantees equality to all citizens. Despite this, the daily lives of people in India are far from equal. Earlier discussions on equality in Civics textbooks most often reiterated certain provisions of the Constitution without adequately considering the reality of these in people's lives. This Unit adopts a different approach. It discusses the need for equality through highlighting the inequalities that continue to be practised and experienced by various communities.

The first chapter introduces the learner to Kanta, Omprakash Valmiki and the Ansaris, all of whom experience inequality in different ways. It is through their experiences that we introduce the concept of dignity. The government's role in passing laws and instituting policies is discussed to show that commitment to the alleviation of existing inequalities is a major part of the work that governments undertake. The chapter also briefly introduces an issue of inequality in the United States of America to highlight that this is a global phenomenon and a feature of many democratic countries.

The second chapter of this Unit is Chapter 10 of this book. It ties together the main ideas on equality raised throughout the text. A significant portion of the last chapter is devoted to discussing people's contribution to the fight for equality. This is achieved through focusing on one social movement as well as highlighting creative (writings, songs, poems) ways through which people express their demands for equality.

Both chapters aim to help the learner understand that equality and democracy are dynamic and not static concepts. This dynamism is reflected in the government's passing of new laws and programmes, and in people's movements around various social and economic issues.

Kanta, Omprakash, the Ansaris, and the Tawa Matsya Sangh all have diverse local equivalents. Local situations should be used as a practical reference to make the discussion on underlying concepts more relevant and appropriate. A discussion on equality in the classroom requires empathy as well as a firm commitment on the teacher's part to ensuring that the dignity of all learners be respected.

CHAPTER 1

On Equality

India is a democracy. In the Class VI book, we looked at the key elements of a democratic government. These include people's participation, the resolution of conflict, and equality and justice. Equality is a key feature of democracy and influences all aspects of its functioning. In this chapter you will read more about equality – what it is, why it is important in a democracy, and whether or not everyone is equal in India. Let's begin by looking at Kanta's story.

On election day, Kanta and her friend Sujata are waiting to cast their votes...

Isn't it good Suja that we can all vote as equal citizens of our country? Even Jain Saheb is standing in the line with us!
Yes!

Go on, Kanta – It's your turn now.

I will vote for the candidate who has promised to bring pipe water to our area.

Abdul Rehman
Artisan
Shabnam Bano
Housewife
Gracy Laleng
Consultant
Isaac Laleng
Government officer
Ruksana Mirza
Media person
Yog Raj
Unemployed
Ashok Jain
Industrialist

Afterwards...

We'll see you later, Kanta.
Yes... Namaste Saheb!

Gudia has been running fever and I have to take her to the hospital...but I will have to finish the work at Saheb's house first...and ask for some advance...

At home...

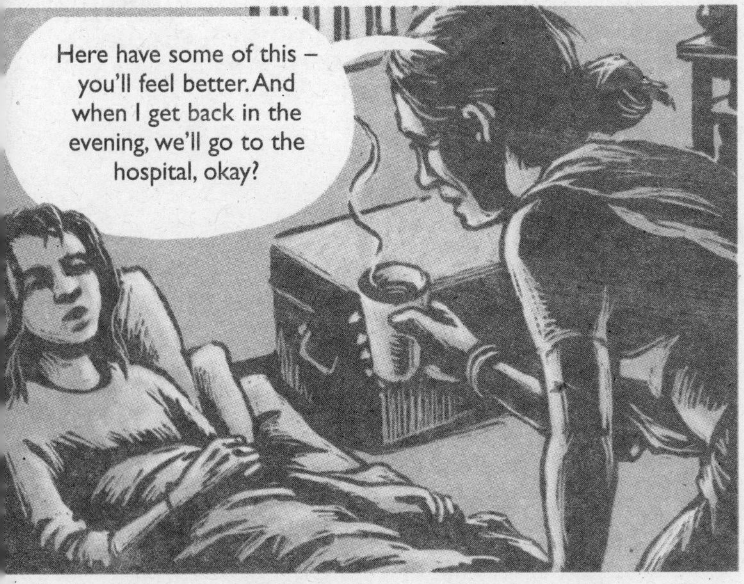
Here have some of this – you'll feel better. And when I get back in the evening, we'll go to the hospital, okay?

It's no wonder that Gudia falls ill often...the *basti* is never cleaned!

That evening...

Equal right to vote

The story above begins with Kanta standing in line to cast her vote. Look again at the various people who are standing in line with her. Kanta recognises her employer, Ashok Jain and Chotte Lal, her neighbour. In a democratic country, like India, all adults irrespective of what religion they belong to, how much education they have had, what caste they are, or whether they are rich or poor are allowed to vote. This, as you have already read in the Class VI book, is called **universal adult franchise** and is an essential aspect of all democracies. The idea of universal adult franchise is based on the idea of equality because it states that every adult in a country, irrespective of their wealth and the communities she/he belongs to, has one vote. Kanta is excited to vote and happy that she is equal to all of the others because each of them has one vote.

But as her day goes on, Kanta becomes less certain about what this equality really means.

What is it that makes Kanta unsure? Let's take a look at a day in her life. She lives in a slum and has a drain behind her house. Her daughter is sick but she cannot take the day off from work because she needs to borrow money from her employers to take her child to the doctor. Her job as a domestic help tires her out, and finally she ends her day by again standing in a long line. This line, in front of the government hospital, is unlike the one in the morning because most of the people standing in it are poor.

Do you think Kanta has enough reason to doubt whether she really is equal? List three reasons from the story above that might make her feel like this.

Other kinds of equality

Kanta is one of many people who live in democratic India and who have the right to vote but whose daily living and working conditions are far from equal. Apart from being poor, people in India experience inequality in different ways. Let us see what this means by reading the two stories given below. Each of these is based on real incidents in people's lives and reflects the different kinds of inequalities that exist in India.

One of the more common forms of inequality in India is the caste system. If you live in rural India your caste identity is something that you probably learned or experienced very young. If you live in urban India some of you might think that people no longer believe in caste. But just look at these matrimonials shown from a leading English newspaper and you will see how important the issue of caste continues to be in the minds of highly educated urban Indians.

Now let us read a story about the experiences of a *Dalit* child attending school. You have already read about Dalits in the Class VI book. *Dalit* is a term that the so-called lower castes use to address themselves. *Dalit* means 'broken' and by using this word, lower castes are pointing to how they were, and continue to be, seriously discriminated against.

Omprakash Valmiki is a famous *Dalit* writer. In his autobiography, *Joothan*, he writes, "I had to sit away from the others in the class, and that too on the floor. The mat ran out before reaching the spot I sat on. Sometimes I would have to sit way behind everybody, right near the door...sometimes they would beat me without any reason." When he was in Class IV, the headmaster asked Omprakash to sweep the school and the playground. He writes, "The playground was way larger than my small physique could handle and in cleaning it, my back began to ache. My face was covered with dust. Dust had gone

✔ **ALLIANCE** invited for 32/MMS/5'4"/fair/b'ful girl working in IT Co. Mumbai from BE / MBA boy working in Mumbai/Abroad from IT Industry Caste no bar. SC/ ST excuse. Send BHP (must)

PROF Qlfd B'ful tall girl 4 Gupta Boy 28/6' CA Working MNC TXS USA $ 80k.

TAMIL BRAHMIN Iyengar groom, 1981 born, Naithruvakashyapa Gothram, Swathi Star, 180cms, tall, fair

Circle the reference to caste in the matrimonial advertisements given above.

Cover of Omprakash Valmiki's book, Joothan, *which talks about his experiences of growing up as a Dalit boy.*

Why do you think Omprakash Valmiki was being treated unequally by his teacher and his classmates? Imagine yourself as Omprakash Valmiki and write four lines about how you would feel if you were in the same situation as him.

Why do you think the Ansaris were being treated unequally? What would you do if you were in the Ansaris' position and could not find a place to live because some people did not want to live next to you because of the religion you practice?

inside my mouth. The other children in my class were studying and I was sweeping. Headmaster was sitting in his room and watching me. I was not even allowed to get a drink of water. I swept the whole day,...From the doors and windows of the school rooms, the eyes of the teachers and the boys saw this spectacle." Omprakash was made to sweep the school and the playground for the next couple of days and this only came to an end when his father, who happened to be passing by, saw his son sweeping. He confronted the teachers and then walking away from the school holding Omprakash's hand, he said loudly for all of them to hear, "You are a teacher...So I am leaving now. But remember this much Master...(He) will study right here...in this school. And not just him, but there will be more coming after him."

The second story is based on an incident that took place in one of India's larger cities and is common practice in most parts of the country. It is a story about Mr and Mrs Ansari who were looking to rent an apartment in the city. They had the money and so paying the rent was no problem. They went to a property dealer for help to find a place. The dealer informed them that he knew about quite a few apartments that were available for rent. They visited the first apartment and the Ansaris liked it very much and decided to take it. However, when the landlady found out their names, she made an excuse about how she could not rent the house to someone who ate meat because the building did not have any non-vegetarian residents. Both the Ansaris and the property dealer were surprised to hear this because they could smell fish being cooked in the neighbour's house. The same excuse was repeated in the second and the third apartments. Finally, the property dealer told them that they might want to change their names and call themselves Mr and Mrs Kumar. The Ansaris were reluctant to do this and decided to look some more. In the end, it took a whole month of looking at apartments before they found a landlady who was willing to give them a place on rent.

Recognising dignity

You have understood by now that the caste we are born into, the religion we practice, the class background we come from, whether we are male or female – these are often the things that determine why some people are treated unequally. Omprakash Valmiki and the Ansaris are being treated unequally on the basis of differences of caste and religion.

When persons are treated unequally, their **dignity** is violated. The dignity of both Omprakash Valmiki and the Ansaris was violated because of the way in which they were treated. By picking on him and making him sweep the school, because of his caste, Omprakash Valmiki's schoolmates and teachers hurt his dignity badly and made him feel as if he was less than equal to all other students in the school. Being a child, Omprakash Valmiki could do very little about the situation that he was in. It was his father who, on seeing his son sweep, felt angry by this unequal treatment and confronted the teachers. The Ansaris' dignity was also hurt when persons refused to lease their apartments to them. However, when the property dealer suggested that they change their name, it was their dignity or self-respect that made them refuse this suggestion.

Omprakash and the Ansaris do not deserve to be treated like this. They deserve the same respect and dignity as anyone else.

Equality in Indian democracy

The Indian **Constitution** recognises every person as equal. This means that every individual in the country, including male and female persons from all castes, religions, tribes, educational and economic backgrounds are recognised as equal. This is not to say that inequality ceases to exist. It doesn't. But atleast, in democratic India, the principle of the equality of all persons is recognised. While earlier

If you were one of the Ansaris how would you have responded to the suggestion that you change your name?

Can you think of an incident in your life in which your dignity was violated? How did this make you feel?

In the 1975 film, Deewar, *a boy who works as a shoeshine refuses to pick up a coin thrown at him. He feels that there is dignity in the work that he does and insists that his fee be given respectfully.*

The Parliament is the cornerstone of our democracy and we are represented in it through our elected representatives.

no law existed to protect people from discrimination and ill-treatment, now there are several that work to see that people are treated with dignity and as equals.

This recognition of equality includes some of the following provisions in the Constitution: first that every person is equal before the law. What this means is that every person, from the President of the country to Kanta, a domestic worker, has to obey the same laws. Second, no person can be discriminated against on the basis of their religion, race, caste, place of birth or whether they are female or male. Third, every person has access to all public places including playgrounds, hotels, shops and markets. All persons can use publicly available wells, roads and bathing ghats. Fourth, untouchability has been abolished.

The two ways in which the government has tried to implement the equality that is guaranteed in the Constitution is first through laws and second through government programmes or schemes to help disadvantaged communities. There are several laws in India that protect every person's right to be treated equally. In addition to laws, the government has also set up several schemes to improve the lives of communities and individuals who have been treated unequally for several centuries. These schemes are to ensure greater opportunity for people who have not had this in the past.

One of the steps taken by the government includes the midday meal scheme. This refers to the programme introduced in all government elementary schools to provide children with cooked lunch. Tamil Nadu was the first state in India to introduce this scheme, and in 2001, the Supreme Court asked all state governments to begin this programme in their schools within six months. This programme has had many positive effects. These include the fact that more poor children have begun enrolling and regularly attending school. Teachers reported that earlier children would often go home for lunch and then not return to school but now with the midday meal being provided in school, their attendance has improved. Their mothers, who earlier had to interrupt their work to feed their children at home during the day, now no longer need to do so. This programme has also helped reduce caste prejudices because both lower and upper caste children in the school eat this meal together, and in quite a few places, *Dalit* women have been employed to cook the meal. The midday meal programme also helps reduce the hunger of poor students who often come to school and cannot concentrate because their stomachs are empty.

While government programmes play an important role in increasing equality of opportunity, there is much that still needs to be done. While the midday meal programme has helped increase the enrolment and attendance of poor children in school, there continues to be big differences in our country between schools that the rich attend and those that the poor attend. Even today there are several schools in the country in which *Dalit* children, like Omprakash Valmiki, are discriminated against and treated unequally. These children are forced into unequal situations in which their dignity is not

Children being served their midday meal at a government school in Uttarakhand.

What is the midday meal programme? Can you list three benefits of the programme? How do you think this programme might help promote greater equality?

Find out about one government scheme in your area. What does this scheme do? Whom is this scheme set up to benefit?

"It is disgraceful to live at the cost of one's self-respect. Self-respect is the most vital factor in life. Without it, man is a cipher. To live worthily with self-respect, one has to overcome difficulties. It is out of hard and ceaseless struggle alone that one derives strength, confidence and recognition.

"Man is mortal. Everyone has to die some day or the other. But one must resolve to lay down one's life in enriching the noble ideals of self-respect and in bettering one's human life... Nothing is more disgraceful for a brave man than to live life devoid of self-respect."

– B.R. Ambedkar

respected. This is because people refuse to think of them as equal even though the law requires it.

One of the main reasons for this is that attitudes change very slowly. Even though persons are aware that discrimination is against the law, they continue to treat people unequally on the basis of their caste, religion, disability, economic status and because they are women. It is only when people begin to believe that no one is inferior, and that every person deserves to be treated with dignity, that present attitudes can change. Establishing equality in a democratic society is a continuous struggle and one in which individuals as well as various communities in India contribute to and you will read more about this in this book.

Issues of equality in other democracies

You are probably wondering whether India is the only democratic country in which there is inequality and where the struggle for equality continues to exist. The truth is that in many democratic countries around the world, the issue of equality continues to be the key issue around which communities struggle. So, for example, in the United States of America, the African-Americans whose ancestors were the slaves who were brought over from Africa, continue to describe their lives today as largely unequal. This, despite the fact that there was a movement in the late 1950s to push for equal rights for African-Americans. Prior to this, African-Americans were treated extremely unequally in the United States and denied equality through law. For example, when travelling by bus, they either had to sit at the back of the bus or get up from their seat whenever a white person wished to sit.

Rosa Parks was an African-American woman. Tired from a long day at work she refused to give up her seat on a bus to a white man on 1 December 1955. Her refusal that day started a huge agitation against the unequal ways in which African-Americans were

treated and which came to be known as the **Civil Rights Movement**. The Civil Rights Act of 1964 prohibited discrimination on the basis of race, religion or national origin. It also stated that all schools would be open to African–American children and that they would no longer have to attend separate schools specially set up for them. However, despite this, a majority of African–Americans continue to be among the poorest in the country. Most African-American children can only afford to attend government schools that have fewer facilities and poorly qualified teachers as compared to white students who either go to private schools or live in areas where the government schools are as highly rated as private schools.

Rosa Parks, an African–American woman, changed the course of American history with one defiant act.

Excerpt from Article 15 of the Indian Constitution

Prohibition of discrimination on grounds of religion, race, caste, sex or place of birth.

(1) The State shall not discriminate against any citizen on grounds only of religion, race, caste, sex, place of birth or any of them.

(2) No citizen shall, on grounds only of religion, race, caste, sex, place of birth or any of them, be subject to any disability, liability, restriction or condition with regard to –

(a) access to shops, public restaurants, hotels and places of public entertainment;

or

(b) the use of wells, tanks, bathing ghats, roads and places of public resort maintained wholly or partly out of State funds or dedicated to the use of the general public.

Challenge of democracy

No country can be described as being completely democratic. There are always communities and individuals trying to expand the idea of democracy and push for a greater recognition of equality on existing as well as new issues. Central to this is the struggle for the recognition of all persons as equal and for their dignity to be maintained. In this book you will read about how this issue of equality affects various aspects of our daily lives in democratic India. As you read these chapters, think about whether the equality of all persons and their being able to maintain their dignity is upheld.

EXERCISES

1. In a democracy why is universal adult franchise important?

2. Re-read the box on Article 15 and state two ways in which this Article addresses inequality?

3. In what ways was Omprakash Valmiki's experience similar to that of the Ansaris?

4. What do you understand by the term "all persons are equal before the law"? Why do you think it is important in a democracy?

5. The Government of India passed the Disabilities Act in 1995. This law states that persons with disabilities have equal rights, and that the government should make possible their full participation in society. The government has to provide free education and integrate children with disabilities into mainstream schools. This law also states that all public places including buildings, schools, etc., should be accessible and provided with ramps.

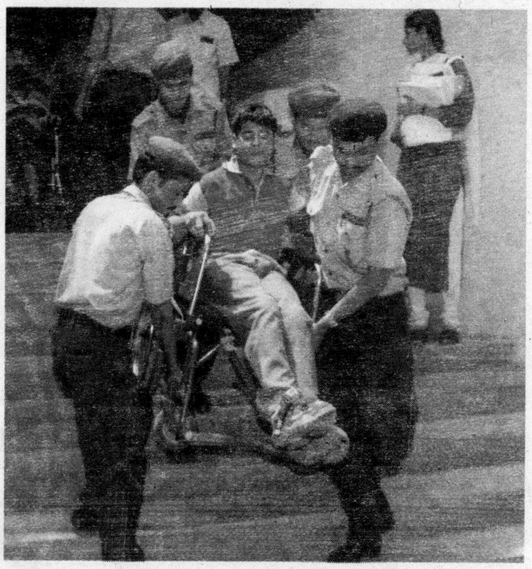

Look at the photograph and think about the boy who is being carried down the stairs. Do you think the above law is being implemented in his case? What needs to be done to make the building more accessible for him? How would his being carried down the stairs affect his dignity as well as his safety?

Glossary

Universal adult franchise: This is a very important aspect of democratic societies. It means that all adult (those who are 18 and above) citizens have the right to vote irrespective of their social or economic backgrounds.

Dignity: This refers to thinking of oneself and other persons as worthy of respect.

Constitution: This is a document that lays down the basic rules and regulations for people and the government in the country to follow.

Civil Rights Movement: A movement that began in USA in 1950s in which African-American people demanded equal rights and an end to racial discrimination.

UNIT TWO

State Government

Teacher's note

These two chapters (Chapters 2 and 3) on State Government are an attempt to discuss the functions and structure of government through concrete situations. We have chosen 'health' as an example; there could have been other, equally important, choices.

Chapter 2 discusses 'health' as an important issue for people. There are both public and private aspects of health provisioning. Healthcare in India is not available to all. While the Constitution supports a view that the right to health is an aspect of our fundamental rights, its provisioning is rather unequal. Through the accounts provided, learners will begin to visualise the ideal or desired role of government, and the meanings behind its structures. Some ways in which this situation can be changed are also discussed.

Chapter 3 focuses on how the government functions, and discusses ideas of representation, accountability and public welfare. Though both the executive and the legislature are presented, one should not expect students to retain fine distinctions. It would be best to patiently encourage them to ask questions such as, "Who is the most powerful person?", "Why can't the MLA solve the problem?", etc. Such queries will enable them to construct a sense of the government apparatus.

It is important that learners acquire the confidence to express their views on public issues and understand the role of government through the exercises given in the chapters. You could choose familiar issues such as water, transport, school-fees, books, child-labour, etc., for them to discuss and arrive at how these problems need to be tackled. Allow them to express these ideas through wall charts. Given that discussions on the government and its functioning often lead to boredom and cynicism, we need to be able to make the classroom session less didactic and more interactive while teaching these lessons.

CHAPTER 2

Role of the Government in Health

In a democracy people expect the government to work for their welfare. This could be through the provision of education, health, employment, housing or the development of roads, electricity etc. In this chapter we shall examine the meanings and problems related to health. Look at the sub-headings of this chapter. In what ways do you think this topic is related to the work of government?

What is health?

We can think of health in many ways. Health means our ability to remain free of illness and injuries. But health isn't only about disease. You may have associated only some of the situations in the above collage with health. What we often ignore is the fact that each of the above situations is related to health. Apart from disease, we need to think of other factors that affect our health. For example, if people get clean drinking water or a pollution free environment they are likely to be healthy. On the other hand, if people do not get adequate food to eat or have to live in cramped conditions, they will be prone to illness.

All of us would like to be active and in good spirits in whatever we may be doing. It isn't healthy to be dull, inactive, anxious or scared for long stretches of time. We all need to be without mental strain. All of these various aspects of our lives are a part of health.

Would you associate all or some of these pictures with 'health' ? In what ways? Discuss in groups.

Pick two situations from the above collage that are not related to illness and write two sentences on how they are related to health.

Healthcare in India

Let us examine some of the aspects of healthcare in India. Compare and contrast the situation expressed in the first and second columns.

Can you provide a title to these columns?

India has the largest number of medical colleges in the world and is among the largest producers of doctors. Approximately 15,000 new doctors qualify every year.	Most doctors settle in urban areas. People in rural areas have to travel long distances to reach a doctor. The number of doctors with respect to the population is much less in rural areas.
Healthcare facilities have grown substantially over the years. In 1950, there were only 2,717 hospitals in India. In 1991, there were 11,174 hospitals. In 2000, the number grew to 18,218.	About five lakh people die from tuberculosis every year. This number is almost unchanged since Independence! Almost two million cases of malaria are reported every year and this number isn't decreasing.
India gets a large number of **medical tourists** from many countries. They come for treatment in some of the hospitals in India that compare with the best in the world.	We are not able to provide clean drinking water to all. 21per cent of all **communicable diseases** are water borne. For example, diarrhoea, worms, hepatitis, etc.
India is the fourth largest producer of medicines in the world and is also a large exporter of medicines.	Half of all children in India do not get adequate food to eat and are undernourished.

In order to prevent and treat illnesses we need appropriate healthcare facilities such as health centres, hospitals, laboratories for testing, ambulance services, blood banks, etc., that can provide the required care and services that patients need. In order to run such facilities we need health workers, nurses, qualified doctors and other health professionals who can advice, diagnose and treat illnesses. We also need the medicines and equipment that are necessary for treating patients. These facilities are required to take care of us.

In India, it is often said that we are unable to provide health services for all because the government does not have enough money and facilities. After reading the above left hand column, do you think this is true? Discuss.

OPD - Out patient deptt.
ICU - Intensive care unit

India has a large number of doctors, clinics and hospitals. The country also has considerable experience and knowledge in running a **public** healthcare system. This is a system of hospitals and health centres run by the government. It has the ability to look after the health of a large section of its population scattered over hundreds of thousands of villages. We will go into more detail on this later. Moreover, there has been a phenomenal advancement in medical sciences whereby many new technologies and treatment procedures are available in the country.

However, the second column points out how poor the health situation in our country is. With all the above positive developments we are not able to provide proper healthcare facilities to people. This is the paradox – something that is contrary to what we would expect. Our country has the money, knowledge and people with experience but cannot make the necessary healthcare available to all. In this chapter, we will look at some of the reasons for this.

Patients usually have to wait in long queues in government hospitals, like this one.

The story of Hakim Seikh

Hakim Seikh was a member of the Paschim Banga Khet Mazdoor Samity (PBKMS), an organisation of agricultural labourers in West Bengal. One evening in 1992, he accidentally fell off a running train and suffered head injuries. He was in a very serious condition and needed immediate treatment.

He was taken to a government hospital in Kolkata but they refused to admit him because they did not have a spare bed. Another hospital did not have the facility or the specialised doctors necessary for his treatment. In this way he spent 14 hours in a critical state and was taken to eight different government hospitals, but none of them admitted him.

Finally, he was admitted in a private hospital, where he received treatment. He spent a lot of money on his treatment. Angry and upset over the indifferent attitude of all the hospitals that refused to admit him, Hakim Seikh and PBKMS filed a case in the court.

*PBKMS. A initiative by Mamta Banerji

Read the story given above. Then imagine that you are a Judge in the court. What would you say to Hakim Seikh?

THE COST OF A CURE

Aman and Ranjan are good friends. While Ranjan comes from a well-to-do family, Aman's parents have to struggle to make ends meet...

Hi Aman! Good to see you back! How have you been?

I had viral fever and had to go to the hospital...
Oh! Me, too! I just got back to school on Monday. My Daddy took me to see the doctor at the new hospital in Kingsway. It was very exciting!

The building looked so posh. I thought it was a five star hotel! Daddy said that was because it was a private hospital, with the best of facilities.

Daddy had to pay Rs 500 at the reception counter itself – before we even met the doctor! There was nice music playing and everything was really clean and shiny.

The doctor asked for many tests...but everyone was so friendly! The lady who took my blood for testing told me so many jokes that I forgot to feel the pain!

After the test results came, we went back to the doctor. He looked through them and said everything was fine, and I only had viral fever. He prescribed some medicines and rest.

...and have you heard the one about Batman on Reality TV?

...and so young man – this pink pill should be taken three times a day, and the white tablet once before bed time – that's for the bodyache! This one is a syrup – don't worry, it's tasty

Thank you Doctor...I feel better already!

You see, I've been dying to tell you all about it! But what about you? Which hospital did you go to?
Um...it wasn't as nice as your's at all! At first, Abba didn't want to take me because he said it would take too much time...

...and it really did! We went to a big Government Hospital. We had to wait in a long queue at the OPD counter. I was feeling so sick that I had to lean on Abba all the time!

When our turn came, the doctor examined me, and asked for a blood test. Then we had to go and stand in another long queue! People were crowding around in the testing room too.

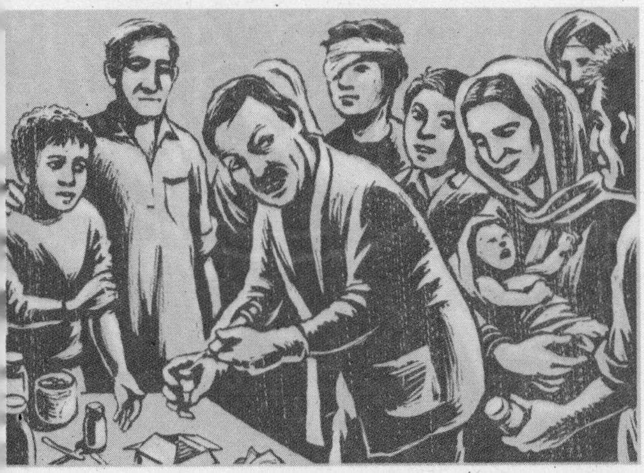

We got the test results after three days...and went back to the hospital. There was a different doctor that day.

Show me his OPD card...and the test results – quickly please!

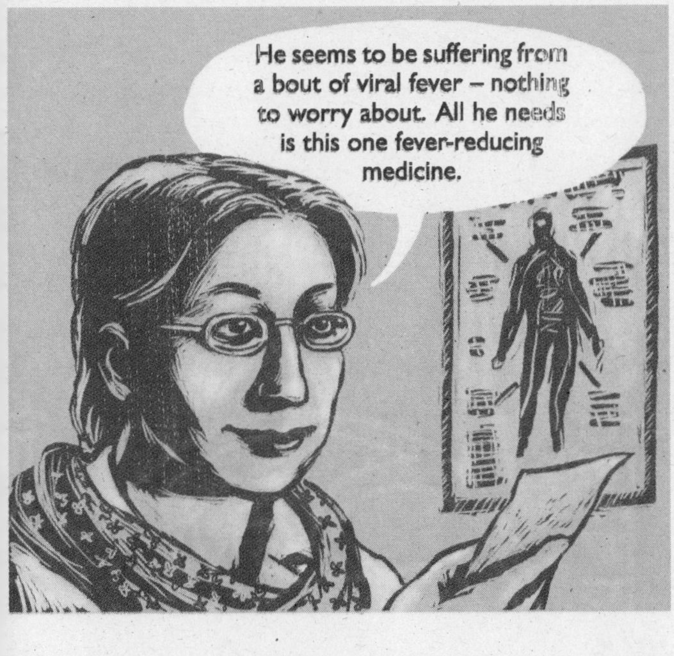

He seems to be suffering from a bout of viral fever – nothing to worry about. All he needs is this one fever-reducing medicine.

My hospital was nice, but they gave me many medicines and the whole thing cost quite a lot!
Oh! My treatment did not cost much!

Where do you go when you are ill? Are there any problems that you face? Write a paragraph based on your experience.

What problems did Aman face in the government hospital? How do you think the hospital can work in a better manner? Discuss.

Why did Ranjan have to spend so much money? Give reasons.

What problems do we face in private hospitals? Discuss.

Why pay taxes to the government?

Government uses tax money for providing many public services for the benefit of all citizens. Some services such as defence, police, judicial system, highways etc. benefit all citizens. Otherwise, the citizens cannot organise these services for themselves.

Taxes fund developmental programmes and services such as education, health care, employment, social welfare, vocational training etc. required for needy citizens. Tax money is utilised for relief and rehabilitation in case of natural disasters such as floods, earthquakes, tsunami etc. Space, nuclear, and missile programmes are also funded from the revenues collected as taxes.

Government provides some services especially for the poor who cannot afford to purchase them from the market. One example is health care. Can you give other examples?

Public and private health care services

From the above story, you must have understood that we can roughly divide up various health care facilities in two categories –

(a) Public health services and

(b) **Private** health facilities.

Public health services

The public health service is a chain of health centres and hospitals run by the government. They are linked together so that they cover both rural and urban areas and can also provide treatment to all kinds of problems – from common illnesses to special services. At the village level there are health centres where there is usually a nurse and a village health worker. They are trained in dealing with common illnesses and work under the supervision of doctors at the Primary Health Centre (PHC). Such a centre covers many villages in a rural area. At the district level is the District Hospital that also supervises all the health centres. Large cities have many government hospitals such as the one where Aman was taken and also specialised government hospitals such as the ones in Hakim Seikh's story.

The health service is called 'public' for many reasons. In order to fulfil its commitment of providing health care to all citizens, the government has established these hospitals and health centres. Also, the resources needed to run these services are obtained from the money that we, the public, pay to the government as taxes. Hence, such facilities are meant for everyone. One of the most important aspects of the public health system is that it is meant to provide quality health care services either free or at a low cost, so that even the poor can seek treatment. Another important function of public health is to take action to prevent the spread of diseases such as TB, malaria, jaundice, cholera, diarrhoea, chikungunya, etc. This has to be organised by the government with the participation of people otherwise it is not effective. For example, when taking up a campaign to see that mosquitoes do not breed in water coolers, rooftops, etc., this has to be done for all houses in the area.

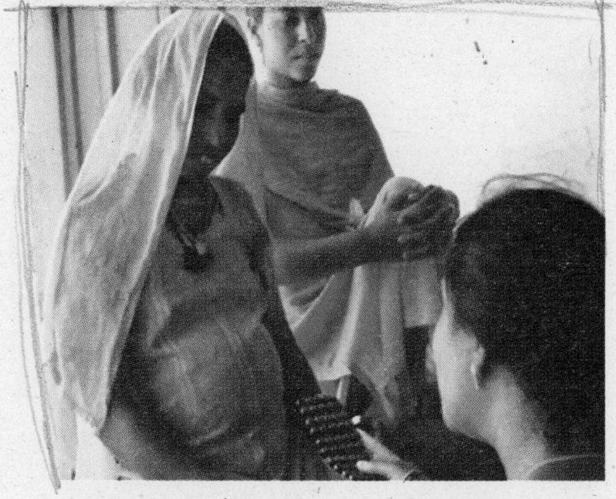

A doctor in a rural health care centre giving medicines to a patient.

Recall the case of Hakim Seikh. Would you like to know what the court said in this case?

According to our Constitution, it is the primary duty of the government to ensure the welfare of the people and provide health care facilities to all.

The government must safeguard the Right to Life of every person. The Court said that the difficulty that Hakim Seikh had to face could have cost him his life. If a hospital cannot provide timely medical treatment to a person, it means that this protection of life is not being given.

The Court also said that it was the duty of the government to provide the necessary health services, including treatment in emergency situations. Hospitals and medical staff must fulfil their duty of providing the necessary treatment. Hakim Seikh was denied treatment at various government hospitals. Therefore, the Court asked the State Government to give him the money that he had spent on his treatment.

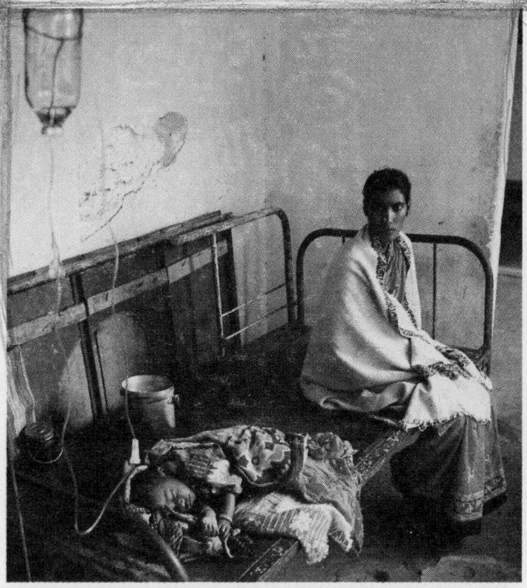

A woman and her sick child at a government hospital. According to UNICEF, more than two million children die every year in India from preventable infections.

Private health facilities

There is a wide range of private health facilities that exist in our country. A large number of doctors run their own private clinics. In the rural areas, one finds Registered Medical Practitioners (RMPs). Urban areas have a large number of doctors, many of them providing specialised services. There are hospitals and nursing homes that are privately owned. There are many laboratories that do tests and offer special facilities such as X-ray, ultrasound, etc. There are also shops from where we buy medicines.

In what ways is the public health system meant for everyone?

List some Primary Health Centres (PHCs) or hospitals near your place. From your experience (or by visiting any one of them), find out the facilities provided and people who run the centre.

* A UN programme well known as UNICEF

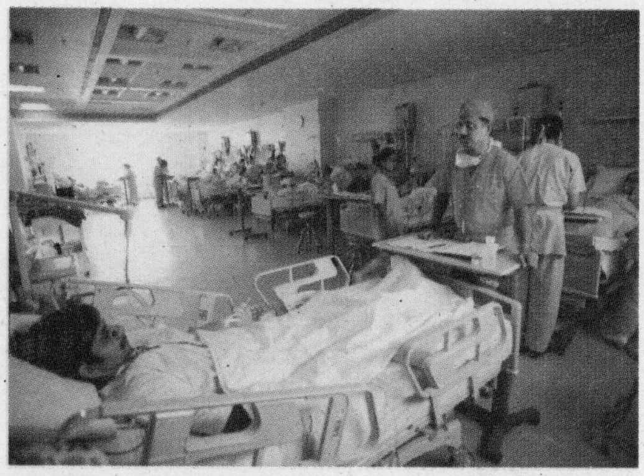

A post-operative room in a leading private hospital in Delhi.

As the name suggests, private health facilities are not owned or controlled by the government. Unlike the public health services, in private facilities, patients have to pay a lot of money for every service that they use.

Today the presence of private facilities can be seen all around. In fact now there are large companies that run hospitals and some are engaged in manufacturing and selling medicines. Medical shops are found in every corner of the country.

Healthcare and equality: Is adequate healthcare available to all?

Private health facilities can mean many things. Explain with the help of some examples from your area.

In India, we face a situation where private services are increasing but public services are not. What is then available to people are mainly private services. These are concentrated in urban areas. The cost of these services is rather high. Medicines are expensive. Many people cannot afford them or have to borrow money when there is an illness in the family.

> The Medical Council of India's Code of Medical **Ethics** states: "Every physician should, as far as possible, prescribe drugs with **generic names** and he/she shall ensure that there is a rational prescription and use of drugs."

Some private services encourage incorrect practices to earn more. At times inexpensive alternatives, though available, may not be used. For example, some medical practitioners are found to prescribe superfluous medicines, injections or saline when simple medication may suffice.

In fact, barely 20 per cent of the population can afford all the medicines that they require during an

How can health care be made more affordable? Discuss.

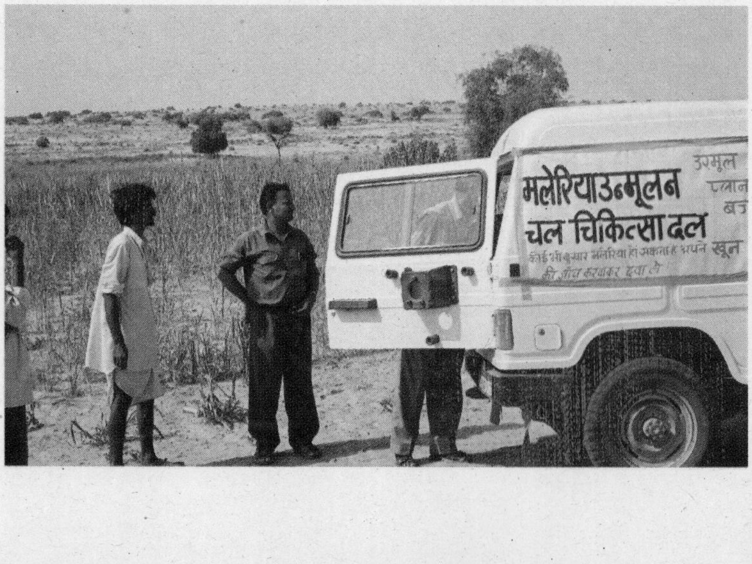

In rural areas, a jeep is often used to serve as a mobile clinic for patients.

illness. Hence, even for those whom one might not think as being poor, medical expenses cause hardship. It was reported in a study that 40 per cent of people who are admitted to a hospital for some illness or injury have to borrow money or sell some of their possessions to pay for the expenses.

This pregnant lady has to travel many kilometres to see a qualified doctor.

For those who are poor, every illness in the family is a cause of great anxiety and distress. What is worse is that this situation tends to happen again and again. Those who are poor are in the first place undernourished. These families are not eating as much as they should. They are not provided basic necessities like drinking water, adequate housing, clean surroundings, etc., and therefore, are more likely to fall ill. The expenses on illness make their situation even worse.

Sometimes it is not only the lack of money that prevents people from getting proper medical treatment. Women, for example, are not taken to a doctor in a prompt manner. Women's health concerns are considered to be less important than the health of men in the family. Many tribal areas have few health centres and they do not run properly. Even private health services are not available.

What can be done?

There is little doubt that the health situation of most people in our country is not good. It is the responsibility of the government to provide quality healthcare services to all its citizens, especially the poor and the disadvantaged. However, health is as much dependent on basic amenities and social conditions of the people, as it is on healthcare services. Hence, it is important to work on both in order to improve the health situation of our people. And this can be done. Look at the following example–

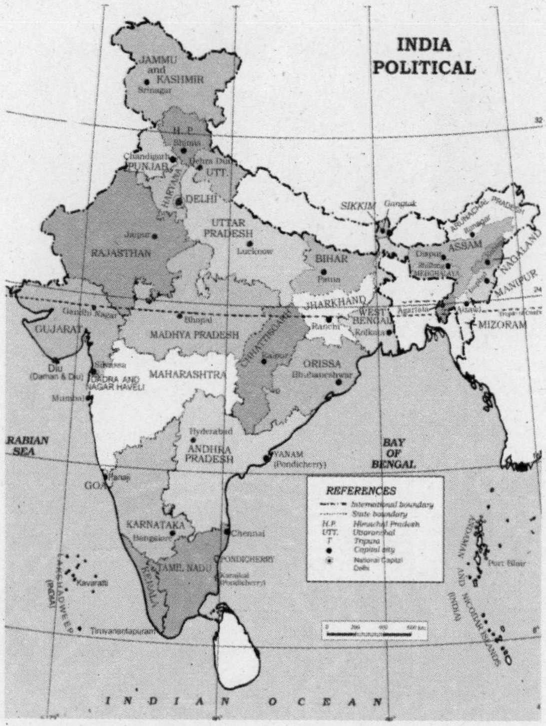

* *Telangana became the 29th State of India on the 2nd June 2014, after the reorganisation of the State of Andhra Pradesh.*

The above map of India shows the state of Kerala in pink.

page 123 of this book has a map of India. Using your pencil outline the state of Kerala on this map.

The Kerala experience

In 1996, the Kerala government made some major changes in the state. Forty per cent of the entire state budget was given to panchayats. They could plan and provide for their requirements. This made it possible for a village to make sure that proper planning was done for water, food, women's development and education. This meant that water supply schemes were checked, the working of schools and *anganwadis* was ensured and specific problems of the village were taken up. Health centres were also improved. All of this helped to improve the situation. Despite these efforts, however, some problems – such as shortage of medicines, insufficient hospital beds, not enough doctors – remained, and these needed to be addressed.

Let us look at an example of another country and its approach to issues of health.

The Costa Rican approach

Costa Rica is considered to be one of the healthiest countries in South America. The main reason for this can be found in the Costa Rican Constitution. Several years ago, Costa Rica took a very important decision and decided not to have an army. This helped the Costa Rican government to spend the money that the army would have used, on health, education and other basic needs of the people. The Costa Rican government believes that a country has to be healthy for its development and pays a lot of attention to the health of its people. The Costa Rican government provides basic services and amenities to all Costa Ricans. For example, it provides safe drinking water, sanitation, nutrition and housing. Health education is also considered very important and knowledge about health is an essential part of education at all levels.

EXERCISES

1. In this chapter you have read that health is a wider concept than illness. Look at this quote from the Constitution and explain the terms 'living standard' and 'public health' in your own words.

An important part of the Constitution says it is the "duty of the State to raise the level of nutrition and the standard of living and to improve public health."

2. What are the different ways through which the government can take steps to provide healthcare for all? Discuss.

3. What differences do you find between private and public health services in your area? Use the following table to compare and contrast these.

Facility	Affordability	Availability	Quality
Private			
Public			

4. 'Improvement in water and sanitation can control many diseases.' Explain with the help of examples.

Glossary

Public: An activity or service that is meant for all people in the country and is mainly organised by the government. This includes schools, hospitals, telephone services, etc. People can demand these services and also raise questions about their non-functioning.

Private: An activity or service that is organised by an individual or company for their own gain.

Medical tourists: This refers to foreigners who come to this country specifically for medical treatment at hospitals that offer world-class facilities at a lower cost than what they would have to pay in their own countries.

Communicable diseases: These are diseases that are spread from one person to another in many ways such as through water, food , air, etc.

OPD: This is the short form for 'Out Patient Department'. This is where people are first brought in and treated in a hospital without being admitted to any special ward.

Ethics: Moral principles that influence a person's behaviour

Generic names: These are chemical names of the drugs. They help in identifying the ingredients. They are globally recognised. For example, acetyl salicylic acid is the generic name of Aspirin.

CHAPTER 3

How the State Government Works

Last year, we discussed the fact that government works at three levels - local, state and national - and looked at the work of local government in some detail. In this chapter, we examine the work of the government at the state level. How does this take place in a democracy? What is the role of a Member of the Legislative Assembly (MLA) and Ministers? How do people express their views or demand action from government? We look at these questions through the example of health.

WHOSE RESPONSIBILITY?

Hey, look at this...it says that there is a water shortage in our state, and people are falling sick!

"...In many villages, people were found to be drinking unclean water. Streams have dried up, and so have tanks. In the worst-affected areas, villagers have been carrying water across great distances."

"People at the district HQ Patalpuram receive water supply once in three days. The District Hospital here is overflowing with patients – a large number of whom are children with acute diarrhoea..."

On the TV news, they said ten people have died from diarrhoea! Is that possible? Can one really die from it?
Who knows? Just hope I don't get it!
That afternoon...
My mother said not to have any iced drinks from the market. She gave one of her lectures this morning, "You have to be responsible for your health, Shirin!"
Ha ha!
Suddenly...
STOP!
This road is blocked due to the rally. They have *gheraoed* the MLA's residence.
Really! Why? Has he done something?
Ha ha – they seem more angry about what he hasn't done!
...and we demand that the authorities take immediate action to bring the public health situation under control! Our MLA must take the responsibility for this!
What a loud voice he has...he must be a leader or something...
Shh...I saw him on TV too. He is a member of the Opposition!

Who is an MLA?

In the above section, you have read about some events in Patalpuram. You may be familiar with some official names such as Collector, Medical Officer, etc. But have you heard of an MLA and the Legislative Assembly? Do you know the MLA of your area? Can you identify which party she or he belongs to?

Members of the Legislative Assembly (MLAs) are elected by the people. They then become members of the legislative assembly and also form the

What is happening in Patalpuram ?

Why is this problem serious?

What action do you think can be taken in the above situation and who do you think should take this action? Discuss.

Discuss the following terms with your teacher-public meeting, States in India, constituency, majority, ruling party and opposition.

Can you explain the following terms-majority, ruling party, opposition with reference to your state.

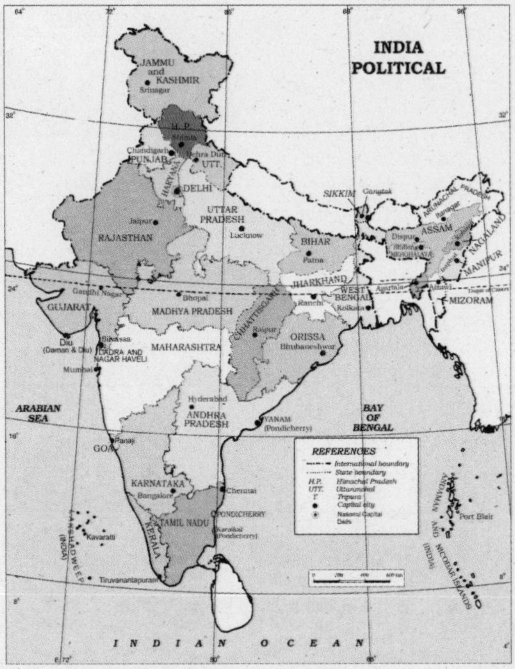

** Telangana became the 29th State of India on the 2nd June 2014, after the reorganisation of the State of Andhra Pradesh.*

The state of Himachal Pradesh is coloured in green in the above thumbnail map of India.

Using a pencil outline the following on the map given on page 123:

(i) the state that you live in;

(ii) the state of Himachal Pradesh.

government. In this way we say that the MLAs represent people. The example below will help us understand this better.

Every state in India has a Legislative Assembly. Each state is divided into different areas or constituencies. For example, look at the map below. It shows that the state of Himachal Pradesh is divided into 68 assembly constituencies. From each **constituency**, the people elect one representative who then becomes a Member of the Legislative Assembly (MLA). You would have noticed that people stand for elections in the name of different parties. These MLAs, therefore, belong to different political parties.

How do people who are MLAs become ministers or chief minister? A political party whose MLAs have won more than half the number of constituencies in a state can be said to be in a **majority**. The political party that has the majority is called the ruling party and all other members are called the **opposition**. For example, the Legislative Assembly of the state of Himachal Pradesh has 68 MLA constituencies.

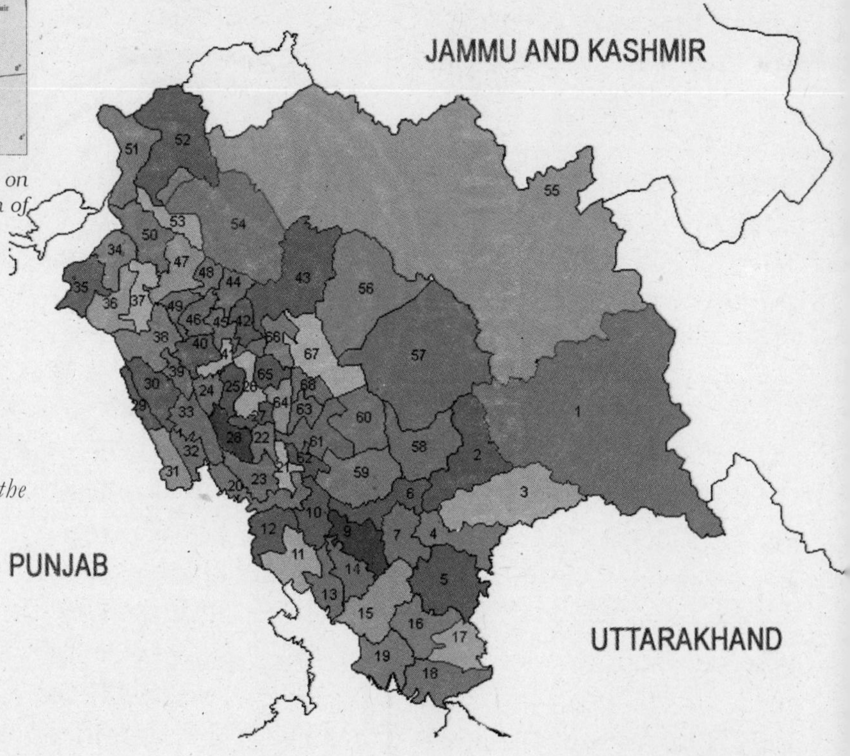

Results of the Assembly Elections in H.P. in 2003

Political party	Number of MLAs elected
Indian National Congress (INC)	43
Bharatiya Janata Party (BJP)	16
Other political parties	03
Independents (who don't belong to any party)	06
Total	**68**

Candidates from various political parties won the 2003 assembly elections and became MLAs. Since the total number of MLAs in the Legislative Assembly is 68, a political party would have needed to have more than 34 MLAs in order to gain a majority. The Indian National Congress with 43 MLAs had the majority and it became the ruling party. All other MLAs became the opposition. In this case, Bharatiya Janata Party was the major opposition party, since it had the largest number of MLAs after the Indian National Congress. Among the opposition were other parties, including those who had been elected as independent candidates.

Construct a table, similar to the one given for Himachal Pradesh, for your state.

The Head of the State is the Governor. She/He is appointed by the Central Government to ensure that the State Government works within the rules and regulations of the Constitution.

After the elections, the MLAs belonging to the ruling party will elect their leader who will become the chief minister. In this case, the Congress Party MLAs chose Shri Virbhadra Singh as their leader and he became the chief minister. The chief minister then selects other people as ministers. After the elections, it is the Governor of the state who appoints the chief minister and other ministers.

At times, the ruling party may not be a single party but a group of parties working together. This is called a coalition. Discuss with your teacher.

The chief minister and other ministers have the responsibility of running various government departments or ministries. They have separate offices. A Legislative Assembly is a place where all the MLAs, whether from the ruling party or from the opposition meet to discuss various things. Hence, some MLAs have dual responsibilities: one as an MLA and the other as a minister. We will read about this further.

A debate in the Legislative Assembly

Afreen, Sujata and many other students from their school travelled to the state capital to visit the Legislative Assembly which was housed in an impressive building. The children were excited. After security checks, they were taken upstairs. There was a gallery from where they could see the large hall below. There were rows and rows of desks.

This Assembly was going to have a debate on a current problem. During this time, MLAs can express their opinions and ask questions related to the issue or give suggestions about what should be done by the government. Those who wish to, can respond to this. The minister then replies to the questions and tries to assure the Assembly that adequate steps are being taken.

The chief minister and other ministers have to take decisions and run the government. We usually hear about them or see them in the news channels or in the papers. However, whatever decisions are being taken have to be approved by the members of the legislative assembly. In a democracy, these members can ask questions, debate an important issue, decide where money should be spent, etc. They have the main authority.

MLA 1: In my constituency of Akhandagaon, during the last three weeks, there were 15 deaths because of diarrhoea. I think it is a shame that this government has not been able to check the situation of a simple problem like diarrhoea while proclaiming itself to be a champion of technology. I would call the attention of the minister in charge of health to take immediate measures to control the situation.

MLA 2: My question is why are government hospitals in such a bad situation? Why is the government not appointing proper doctors and other medical staff in the district? I would also like to know how the government plans to deal with this situation which is affecting a large number of people and is also spreading. This is an epidemic.

MLA 3: My constituency of Tolpatti too has a serious shortage of water. Women travel up to 3 or 4 kilometres to collect water. How many tankers have been put into service to supply water? How many wells and ponds have been cleaned and disinfected?

MLA 4: I think my colleagues are exaggerating the problem. The government has taken steps to control the situation. Water tankers have been put into service. ORS packets are being distributed. The government is doing everything possible to help people.

MLA 5: We have very poor facilities in our hospitals. There are hospitals that do not have a doctor and no medical staff has been appointed for the last few years. In another hospital, the doctor has gone on a long leave. This is a shame. I think the situation is going from bad to worse. How are we going to ensure that ORS packets reach all families in the affected areas?

MLA 6: The opposition members are unnecessarily blaming the government. The previous government did not pay any attention to sanitation. We have now taken up a drive to clear the garbage that has been lying around for years.

Can you identify the MLAs of the ruling party and the opposition in the illustration? Colour the ruling party in one colour and the opposition in another.

What were the main arguments put forward by different MLAs who thought that the government was not taking the situation in a serious manner?

If you were the health minister, how would you respond to the above discussion?

Do you think the above debate would have been useful in some ways? How? Discuss.

In the working of the government, explain the difference between being an MLA and an MLA who is also a minister.

In the earlier section you have read about a debate in the Legislative Assembly. The members were debating the action taken or not taken by the government. This is because the MLAs are together responsible for the work of the government. In common usage the word 'government' refers to government departments and various ministers who head them. The overall head is the chief minister. More correctly, this is called the executive part of the government. All the MLAs who gather together (assemble) in the legislative assembly are called the Legislature. They are the ones who authorise and supervise their work. As we saw in the earlier section, it is from among them that the head of the executive, or the chief minister is formed.

Working of the government

The Legislative Assembly is not the only place where opinions are expressed about the work of the government and action is demanded. You will find newspapers, TV channels and other organisations regularly talking about the government. In a democracy, there are various ways through which people express their views and also take action. Let us look at one such way.

Soon after the discussion in the assembly, there was a **press conference** organised by the health minister. Large numbers of people from different newspapers were present. The minister and some government officials were also present. The minister explained the steps the government had taken. Reporters asked many questions at this meeting. These discussions were then reported in different newspapers. The following page has one such report.

During the next week, the chief minister and the minister for health visited Patalpuram district. They went to visit the families who had lost their relatives and also visited people in the hospitals. The government announced a compensation for these

Government smells the garbage

Chief Minister promises funds for work

Patalpuram | Ravi Ahuja

During the last few weeks, there have been many deaths in some districts of our state. There has been a strong reaction that the government has not taken this seriously. The health minister explained today at a press conference that his government has asked all the collectors and the chief medical officers to take urgent measures. The most important problem is that of drinking water. The minister said that they intend to supply drinking water to every village through tanker trucks. The chief minister has promised funds for this work. They also plan to start a campaign to inform people about the steps that can be taken to prevent diarrhoea. When a reporter asked him as to what steps are being taken to see that garbage that has been lying around for months is quickly collected, the chief minister said that he would look into this.

Write two measures that the goverment undertook for controlling diarrhoea?

What is the purpose of a press conference? How does the press conference help you get information on what the goverment is doing?

families. The chief minister also said that he thought the problem was not only one of sanitation but also of a lack of clean drinking water. He said that a high-level enquiry committee will be asked to look into the needs of the district to provide sanitation facilities and would request the minister for Public Works to take care of the needs of proper water supply in the region.

As you saw above, the people in power like the chief minister and the minister have to take action. They do so through various departments like the Public Works Department, the Agriculture Department, the Health Department, the Education Department and so on. They also have to answer questions that are asked in the Legislative Assembly and convince people asking the questions that proper steps are being taken. At the same time, newspapers and the media widely discuss the issue and the government has to respond, for example, by holding the press conferences.

The government can also decide to make new laws for the state regarding sanitation and health facilities. For example, it may make it compulsory for municipal corporations to ensure that there are adequate toilets in every urban area. It may also ensure that a health worker is appointed in every village. This act of making laws on certain issues is done in the Legislative Assembly of each state. The various government departments then implement these laws. Laws for the entire country are made in the Parliament. You will read more about the Parliament next year.

In a democracy, it is the people who elect their representatives as Members of the Legislative Assembly (MLAs) and, thus, it is the people who have the main authority. The ruling party members then form the government and some members are appointed ministers. These ministers are in charge of various departments of the government such as health in the above example. Whatever work is done by these departments has to be approved by the members of the legislative assembly.

In a democracy, people organise meetings to voice their opinions and protest against the government.

Name of department	Examples of their work
School Education	
Public Works Department	
Agriculture	

Find out with the help of your teacher, the work done by the government departments mentioned above, and fill in the table.

A wallpaper project

A wallpaper is an interesting activity through which research can be done on particular topics of interest. The following photographs explain the different aspects involved in creating a wallpaper in a classroom.

After introducing the topic and having a brief discussion with the whole class, the teacher divides the class into groups. The group discusses the issue and decides what it would like to include in the wall-paper. Children then work individually or in pairs to read the collected material and write their observations or experiences. They can do this through creating stories, poems, case studies, interviews, etc.

The group looks at the material that they have selected, drawn or written. They read each other's writing and provide feedback to each other. They make decisions on what should be included and finalise the layout for the wallpaper.

Each group then presents the wallpaper to the entire class. It is important that more than one member of the group is asked to present and that each group is allotted the same amount of time to discuss their work. After each group has presented, it would be a good idea to have a feedback session on the following– What more could they do on their own? How could their work be organised better? How could writing and presentation be improved upon?

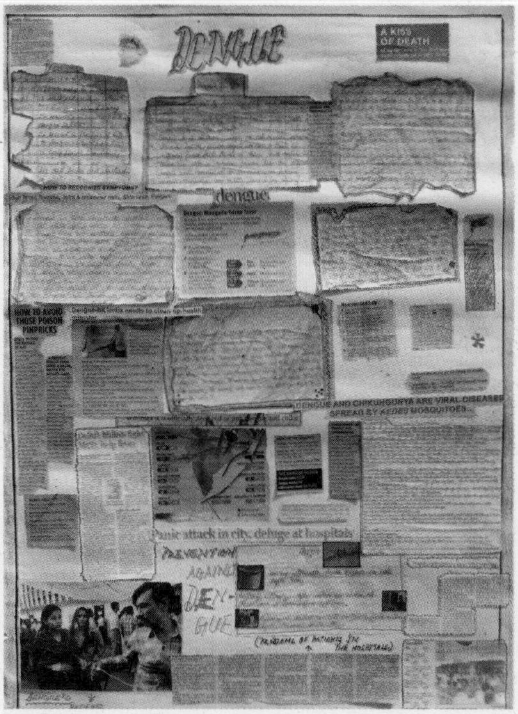

This wallpaper about the 2006 dengue epidemic was prepared by children of Class VI B of Kendriya Vidyalaya II, Hindon, Ghaziabad, Uttar Pradesh.

Do a similar wallpaper project about any issue connected with the working of your State Government like an education programme, any law and order issue, midday meal scheme, etc.

EXERCISES

1. Use the terms 'constituency' and 'represent' to explain who an MLA is and how is the person elected?
2. How did some MLAs become Ministers? Explain.
3. Why should decisions taken by the Chief Minister and other ministers be debated in the Legislative Assembly?
4. What was the problem in Patalpuram? What discussion/ action was taken by the following? Fill in the table.

Public meeting	
Legislative Assembly	
Press conference	
Chief Minister	

5. What is the difference between the work that MLAs do in the Assembly and the work done by government departments?

Glossary

Constituency: A particular area from which all the voters living there choose their representatives. This could be, for example, a panchayat ward or an area that chooses an MLA.

Majority: This is a situation when more than half the number in a group supports a decision or an idea. This is also called a simple majority.

Opposition: This refers to elected representatives who are not members of the ruling party and who play the role of questioning government decisions and actions as well as raise new issues for consideration in the Assembly.

Press Conference: A gathering of journalists from the media who are invited to hear about and ask questions on a particular issue and are then expected to report on this to the larger public.

UNIT THREE

Gender

Teacher's note

Gender is a term that you may often have heard. It is a term, however, that is not easily understood. It tends to remain distant from our lives and restricted to discussions during training programmes. In fact, it is something that all of us experience in our lives on a daily basis. It determines, for example, who we are and what we will become, where we can go and where not, the life choices available to us and those we eventually make. Our understanding of gender is often based on the family and society that we live in. This leads us to think that the roles we see men and women around us play are fixed and natural. In fact, these roles differ across communities around the world. By gender, then, we mean the many social values and stereotypes our cultures attach to the biological distinction 'male' and 'female'. It is a term that helps us to understand many of the inequalities and power relations between men and women in society.

The following two chapters explore the concept of gender without actually using the term. Instead, through different pedagogic tools like case studies, stories, classroom activities, data analysis and photographs, students are encouraged to question and think about their own lives and the society around them. Gender is often mistakenly thought to be something that concerns women or girls alone. Thus, care has been taken in these chapters to draw boys into the discussion as well.

Chapter 4 uses two case studies, situated in different places and points in time to show how girls and boys are brought up or socialised differently. This enables them to understand that the process of socialisation is not uniform; instead it is socially determined and changes continuously over time. The chapter also addresses the fact that societies assign different values to the roles men and women play and the work they do, which becomes a basis for inequality and discrimination. Through a storyboard, students discuss the issue of housework. Done primarily by women, housework is often not considered 'work' and, therefore made invisible and devalued.

Chapter 5 further develops ideas around gender inequalities in the world of work and describes women's struggles for equality. Through a classroom activity, students begin questioning existing stereotypes regarding work and career choices. The chapter also points out that opportunities like education are not equally available to boys and girls. By reading about the lives of two Indian women, from the ninteenth and twentieth centuries, students see how women struggled to change their lives by learning to read and write. Change on a large scale usually takes place through collective struggles. The chapter concludes with a photo-essay that gives examples of different strategies the women's movement has used to fight for change.

CHAPTER 4

Growing up as Boys and Girls

Being a boy or a girl is an important part of one's identity. The society we grow up in teaches us what kind of behaviour is acceptable for girls and boys, what boys and girls can or cannot do. We often grow up thinking that these things are exactly the same everywhere. But do all societies look at boys and girls in the same way? We will try and answer this question in this chapter. We will also look at how the different roles assigned to boys and girls prepare them for their future roles as men and women. We will learn that most societies value men and women differently. The roles women play and the work they do are usually valued less than the roles men play and the work they do. This chapter will also examine how inequalities between men and women emerge in the area of work.

Growing up in Samoa in the 1920s

The Samoan Islands are part of a large group of small islands in the southern part of the Pacific Ocean. In the 1920s, according to research reports on Samoan society, children did not go to school. They learnt many things, such as how to take care of children or do household work from older children and from adults. Fishing was a very important activity on the islands. Young people, therefore, learnt to undertake long fishing expeditions. But they learnt these things at different points in their childhood.

A Class VII Samoan child in his school uniform.

In what ways do the experiences of Samoan children and teenagers differ from your own experiences of growing up? Is there anything in this experience that you wish was part of your growing up?

As soon as babies could walk, their mothers or other adults no longer looked after them. Older children, often as young as five years old, took over this responsibility. Both boys and girls looked after their younger siblings. But, by the time a boy was about nine years old, he joined the older boys in learning outdoor jobs like fishing and planting coconuts. Girls had to continue looking after small children or do errands for adults till they were teenagers. But, once they became teenagers they had much more freedom. After the age of fourteen or so, girls also went on fishing trips, worked in the plantations, learnt how to weave baskets. Cooking was done in special cooking-houses, where boys were supposed to do most of the work while girls helped with the preparations.

Growing up male in Madhya Pradesh in the 1960s

The following is adapted from an account of experiences of being in a small town in Madhya Pradesh in the 1960s.

From Class VI onwards, boys and girls went to separate schools. The girls' school was designed very differently from the boys' school. They had a central courtyard where they played in total seclusion and

Why do girls like to go to school together in groups?

Make a drawing of a street or a park in your neighbourhood. Show the different kinds of activities young boys and girls may be engaged in. You could do this individually or in groups.

Are there as many girls as boys in your drawing? Most probably you would have drawn fewer girls. Can you think of reasons why there are fewer women and girls in your neighbourhood streets, parks and markets in the late evenings or at night?

Are girls and boys doing different activities? Can you think of reasons why this might be so? What would happen if you replaced the girls with the boys and vice-versa?

safety from the outside world. The boys' school had no such courtyard and our playground was just a big space attached to the school. Every evening, once school was over, the boys watched as hundreds of school girls crowded the narrow streets. As these girls walked on the streets, they looked so purposeful. This was unlike the boys who used the streets as a place to stand around idling, to play, to try out tricks with their bicycles. For the girls, the street was simply a place to get straight home. The girls always went in groups, perhaps because they also carried fears of being teased or attacked.

After reading the two examples above, we realise that there are many different ways of growing up. Often we think that there is only one way in which children grow up. This is because we are most familiar with our own experiences. If we talk to elders in our family, we will see that their childhoods were probably very different from ours.

We also realise that societies make clear distinctions between boys and girls. This begins from a very young age. We are for example, given different toys to play with. Boys are usually given cars to play with and girls dolls. Both toys can be a lot of fun to play with. Why are girls then given dolls and boys cars? Toys become a way of telling children that they will have different futures when they become men and women. If we think about it, this difference is created in the smallest and most everyday things. How girls must dress, what games boys should play, how girls need to talk softly or boys need to be tough. All these are ways of telling children that they have specific roles to play when they grow up to be men and women. Later in life this affects the subjects we can study or the careers we can choose.

In most societies, including our own, the roles men and women play or the work they do, are not valued equally. Men and women do not have the same status. Let us look at how this difference exists in the work done by men and women.

'MY MOTHER DOES NOT WORK'

Ma, we are going on a school excursion. Rosie Ma'am needs volunteers. Can't you take a holiday from office and volunteer?

Harmeet's mother always comes for excursions, beause she doesn't work.
Shonali, how can you say that! You know that Jaspreet aunty is up at 5 a.m. everyday doing all the housework!
Yes, but that's not real work, it's just house work!
Oh! That's what you think, do you? Let's go over to their house and ask Jaspreet what she thinks!

the Singh's house

Harsharan, Shonali thinks that your wife is not a working person!
But isn't that correct aunty? My mother is a housewife – she does not work!
Ha, ha!

Then Jaspreet, why don't you just relax and let them manage everything for a change?
Great idea! OK, I'll go on strike tomorrow!
What fun! We'll take care of everything tomorrow – with Papa!

xt morning, 7:30 a.m.

Oh God! Look at the time! here's my breakfast? Why aren't the children ready?
How would I know? I'm on strike, remember? Besides, Mangala has also taken leave today.

Oh-ho! That's the school bus! I'll have to drop them in the car.
HONK
HONK
Hurry, hurry! And ask Harmeet to switch on the pump!

Valuing housework

Harmeet's family did not think that the work Jaspreet did within the house was real work. This feeling is not unique to their families. Across the world, the main responsibility for housework and **care-giving** tasks, like looking after the family, especially children, the elderly and sick members, lies with women. Yet, as we have seen, the work that women do within the home is not recognised as work. It is also assumed that this is something that comes naturally to women. It, therefore, does not have to be paid for. And society **devalues** this work.

Lives of domestic workers

In the story above, Harmeet's mother was not the only one who did the housework. A lot of the work was done by Mangala, their domestic helper. Many homes, particularly in towns and cities, employ domestic workers. They do a lot of work – sweeping and cleaning, washing clothes and dishes, cooking, looking after young children or the elderly. Most domestic workers are women. Sometimes, even young boys or girls are employed to do this work. Wages are low, as domestic work does not have much value. A domestic worker's day can begin as early as five in the morning and end as late as twelve at night! Despite the hard work they do, their employers often do not show them much respect. This is what Melani, a domestic worker had to say about her experience of working in Delhi – *"My first job was with a rich family that lived in a three-storeyed house. The memsahib was very strange as she would shout to get any work done. My work was in the kitchen. There were two other girls who did the cleaning. Our day would begin at 5 o'clock. For breakfast we would get a cup of tea and two dry rotis. We could never get a third roti. In the evening, when I cooked the food, the two other girls would beg me to give them an extra roti. I would secretly give it to them and make an extra one for myself. We were so hungry after working through the day! We could not wear chappals in the house. In the winter, our feet would swell up with the cold. I used to feel scared of the memsahib but also felt angry and humiliated. Did we not work all day? Did we not deserve to be treated with some respect?"*

Melani with her daughter.

Were Harmeet and Shonali correct in saying that Harmeet's mother did not work?

What do you think would happen if your mother or those involved in doing the work at home went on a strike for a day?

Why do you think that men and boys generally do not do housework? Do you think they should?

In fact, what we commonly term as housework actually involves many different tasks. A number of these tasks require heavy physical work. In both rural and urban areas women and girls have to fetch water. In rural areas women and girls carry heavy headloads of firewood. Tasks like washing clothes, cleaning, sweeping and picking up loads require bending, lifting and carrying. Many chores, like cooking, involve standing for long hours in front of hot stoves. The work women do is strenuous and physically demanding — words that we normally associate with men.

Another aspect of housework and care-giving that we do not recognise is that it is very time consuming. In fact, if we add up the housework and the work, women do outside the home, we find that women spend much more time working than men and have much less time for leisure.

Below is some data from a special study done by the Central Statistical Organization of India (1998-1999). See if you can fill in the blanks.

State	Women Paid (Work hours per week)	Women Unpaid (Housework hours per week)	Women (Total)	Men Paid (Work hours per week)	Men Unpaid (Housework hours per week)	Men (Total)
Haryana	23	30	?	38	2	?
Tamil Nadu	19	35	?	40	4	?

What are the total number of work hours spent by women in Haryana and Tamil Nadu each week?

How does this compare with the total number of work hours spent by men?

Many women like Shonali's mother in the story and the women in Tamil Nadu and Haryana who were surveyed work both inside and outside the home. This is often referred to as the ***double burden*** *of women's work.*

Women's work and equality

As we have seen the low value attached to women's household and care-giving work is not an individual or family matter. It is part of a larger system of inequality between men and women. It, therefore, has to be dealt with through actions not just at the level of the individual or the family but also by the government. As we now know, equality is an important principle of our Constitution. The Constitution says that being male or female should not become a reason for discrimination. In reality, inequality between the sexes exists. The government is, therefore, committed to understanding the reasons for this and taking positive steps to remedy the situation. For example, it recognises that burden of child-care and housework falls on women and girls.

Children at an Anganwadi centre in a village in Madhya Pradesh.

This naturally has an impact on whether girls can attend school. It determines whether women can work outside the house and what kind of jobs and careers they can have. The government has set up *anganwadis* or child-care centres in several villages in the country. The government has passed laws that make it mandatory for organisations that have more than 30 women employees to provide crèche facilities. The provision of crèches helps many women to take up employment outside the home. It also makes it possible for more girls to attend schools.

What do you think this poster is trying to say?

मै
हर कही मौजूद
मेरी अनदेखी
और नही संभव
कौन सी
वह तुम्हारी उपलब्धि
जिसमें मेरा नही वह भाग
औरत को चाहिए अपना अधिकार
महिला जागरण केन्द्र, पंचवटी नगर, राजेन्द्र नगर पटना-800 016
असहाय पीड़ित महिला कल्याण संस्था, पच्चखुट्टी, खगड़िया

This poster was created by a women's group in Bengal. Can you write an interesting slogan for the poster?

পাই অপমান,খোঁটা,লাঠি
সচেতনা

EXERCISES

1. Are the statements given alongside true or false. Support your answer with the use of an example -

   a. All societies do not think similarly about the roles that boys and girls play.

   b. Our society does not make distinctions between boys and girls when they are growing up.

   c. Women who stay at home do not work.

   d. The work that women do is less valued than that of men.

2. Housework is *invisible* and unpaid work.

   Housework is *physically demanding.*

   Housework is *time consuming.*

   Write in your own words what is meant by the terms 'invisible', 'physically demanding', and 'time consuming'? Give one example of each based on the household tasks undertaken by women in your home.

3. Make a list of toys and games that boys typically play and another for girls. If there is a difference between the two lists, can you think of some reasons why this is so? Does this have any relationship to the roles children have to play as adults?

4. If you have someone working as a domestic help in your house or locality talk to her and find out a little bit more about her life - Who are her family members? Where is her home? How many hours does she work? How much does she get paid? Write a small story based on these details.

Glossary

Identity: Identity is a sense of self-awareness of who one is. Typically, a person can have several identities. For example, a person can be a girl, a sister and a musician.

Double-burden: Literally means a double load. This term is commonly used to describe the women's work situation. It has emerged from a recognition that women typically labour both inside the home (housework) and outside.

Care-giving: Care-giving refers to a range of tasks related to looking after and nurturing. Besides physical tasks, they also involve a strong emotional aspect.

De-valued: When someone is not given due recognition for a task or job they have done, they can feel de-valued. For example, if a boy has put in a lot of effort into making a special birthday gift for his friend and this friend does not say anything about this, then the boy may feel de-valued.

CHAPTER 5

Women Change the World

In the previous chapter, we saw how women's work in the home is not recognised as work. We also read how doing household work and taking care of family members is a full time job and there are no specific hours at which it begins or ends. In this chapter, we will look at work outside the home, and understand how some occupations are seen to be more suitable for men than for women. We will also learn about how women struggle for equality. Getting an education was, and still is, one way in which new opportunities were created for women. This chapter will also briefly trace the different types of efforts made by the women's movement to challenge discrimination in more recent years.

Who does what work?

Draw images of the following –

farmer

A factory worker

A nurse

scientist

A pilot

A teacher

See what images your class drew by filling in the table below. Add up the number of male and female images separately for each occupation.

Category	Male image	Female image
Teacher		
Farmer		
Factory worker		
Nurse		
Scientist		
Pilot		

Are there more images of men than women?

In what kinds of jobs were there more images of men than women?

Have all the nurses been drawn as females? Why?

Are there fewer images of female farmers? If so, why?

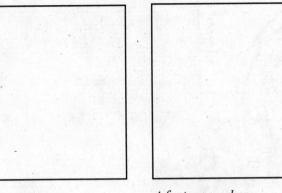

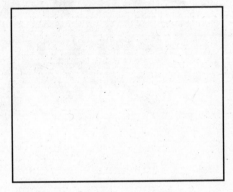

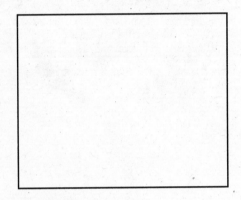

83.6 per cent of working women in India are engaged in agricultural work. Their work includes planting, weeding, harvesting and threshing. Yet, when we think of a farmer we only think of a man.
Source: NSS 61st Round (2004-05)

Rosie Ma'am's class has 30 children. She did the same exercise in her class and here is the result.

Category	Male image	Female image
Teacher	5	25
Farmer	30	0
Factory worker	25	5
Nurse	0	30
Scientist	25	5
Pilot	27	3

How does your class exercise compare with Rosie Ma'am's class exercise?

Fewer opportunities and rigid expectations

A lot of the children in Rosie Ma'am's class drew women as nurses and men as army officers. The reason they did this is because they feel that outside the home too, women are good at only certain jobs. For example, many people believe that women make better nurses because they are more patient and gentle. This is linked to women's roles within the family. Similarly, it is believed that science requires a technical mind and girls and women are not capable of dealing with technical things.

Because so many people believe in these **stereotypes**, many girls do not get the same support that boys do to study and train to become doctors and engineers. In most families, once girls finish school, they are encouraged by their families to see marriage as their main aim in life.

Breaking stereotypes

Engine drivers are men. But 27-year-old Laxmi Lakra, from a poor tribal family in Jharkhand has begun to change things. She is the first woman engine driver for Northern Railways.

Laxmi's parents are not literate but they struggled and overcame many hardships to make sure their children got an education. Laxmi studied in a government school. Even in school, Laxmi helped with the housework and did odd jobs. She studied hard and did well and then went on to get a diploma in electronics. She then took the railway board exam and passed it on her first attempt.

Laxmi says, "I love challenges and the moment somebody says it is not for girls, I make sure I go ahead and do it." Laxmi has had to do this several times in her life – when she wanted to take electronics; when she rode motorcycles at the polytechnic; and when she decided to become an engine driver.

Her philosophy is simple – "As long as I am having fun without harming anyone, as long as I am doing well and helping my parents, why should I not lead a lifestyle of my choice?"

(Adapted from Driving Her Train *by Neeta Lal, Women's Features Service)*

Read the story below and answer the questions -

If you were Xavier, what subject would you choose and why?

In your experience, what are some of the other pressures that boys experience?

It is important to understand that we live in a society in which all children face pressures from the world around them. Sometimes, these come in the form of demands from adults. At other times, they can just be because of unfair teasing by our own friends. Boys are pressurised to think about getting a job that will pay a good salary. They are also teased and bullied if they do not behave like other boys. You may remember that in your Class VI book you read about how boys at an early age are encouraged not to cry in front of others.

Xavier was happy with the results of his Class X board exams. Though his marks in Science and Maths were not high, he had done well in his favourite subjects – History and Languages. When his parents saw his report card, however, they did not look pleased at all...

My Goodness! Xavier, you have managed only 65% in Maths. Your marks in Physics are low too...
I know Mama, but it's okay, because I don't want to take Maths or Science. I want to study History.

Why do you want to take History? Think about your future. You have to get a good job! History will not help. It has no scope!
But, but, I don't like Maths or Science!

Be sensible, son. Take Maths, and you can study computers side by side. The job market for computers is very good.

Ramabai (1858–1922), shown above with her daughter, championed the cause of women's education. She never went to school but learnt to read and write from her parents. She was given the title 'Pandita' because she could read and write Sanskrit, a remarkable achievement as women then were not allowed such knowledge. She went on to set up a Mission in Khedgaon near Pune in 1898, where widows and poor women were encouraged not only to become literate but to be independent. They were taught a variety of skills from carpentry to running a printing press, skills that are not usually taught to girls even today. The printing press can be seen in the picture on the top left corner. Ramabai's Mission is still active today.

Learning for change

Going to school is an extremely important part of your life. As more and more children enter school every year, we begin to think that it is normal for *all* children to go to school. Today, it is difficult for us to imagine that school and learning could be seen as "out of bounds" or not appropriate for some children. But in the past, the skill of reading and writing was known to only a few. Most children learnt the work their families or elders did. For girls, the situation was worse. In communities that taught sons to read and write, daughters were not allowed to learn the alphabet. Even in families where skills like pottery, weaving and craft were taught, the contribution of daughters and women was only seen as supportive. For example, in the pottery trade, women collected the mud and prepared the earth for the pots. But since they did not operate the wheel, they were not seen as potters.

In the nineteenth century, many new ideas about education and learning emerged. Schools became more common and communities that had never learnt reading and writing started sending their children to school. But there was a lot of opposition to educating girls even then. Yet many women and men made efforts to open schools for girls. Women struggled to learn to read and write.

Let us read about the experience of Rashsundari Devi (1800–1890), who was born in West Bengal, some 200 years ago. At the age of 60, she wrote her autobiography in Bangla. Her book titled *Amar Jiban* is the first known autobiography written by an Indian woman. Rashsundari Devi was a housewife from a rich landlord's family. At that time, it was believed that if a woman learnt to read and write, she would bring bad luck to her husband and become a widow! Despite this, she taught herself how to read and write in secret, well after her marriage.

Learning to read and write led some women to question the situation of women in society. They wrote stories, letters and autobiographies describing their own experiences of inequality. In their writings, they also imagined new ways of thinking and living for both men and women.

"I would start working at dawn, and I would still be at it until well beyond midnight. I had no rest in between. I was only fourteen years old at the time. I came to nurture a great longing: I would learn to read and I would read a religious manuscript. I was

Rokeya Sakhawat Hossain and her dreams about 'Ladyland'

Rokeya Sakhawat Hossain was born into a rich family who owned a lot of land. Though she knew how to read and write Urdu, she was stopped from learning Bangla and English. In those days, English was seen as a language that would expose girls to new ideas, which people thought were not correct for them. Therefore, it was mostly boys who were taught English. Rokeya learnt to read and write Bangla and English with the support of her elder brother and an elder sister. She went on to become a writer. She wrote a remarkable story titled *Sultana's Dream* in 1905 to practise her English skills when she was merely 25 years old. This story imagined a woman called Sultana who reaches a place called *Ladyland.* Ladyland is a place where women had the freedom to study, work, and create inventions like controlling rain from the clouds and flying air cars. In this Ladyland, the men had been sent into seclusion – their aggressive guns and other weapons of war defeated by the brain-power of women. As Sultana travels in Ladyland with Sister Sarah, she awakes to realise that she was only dreaming.

As you can see, Rokeya Sakhawat Hossain was dreaming of women flying planes and cars even before girls were being allowed to go to school! This was the way in which education and learning had changed Rokeya's own life. Rokeya did not stop at getting education just for herself. Her education gave her the power not only to dream and write, but also to do more – to help other girls go to school and to build their own dreams. In 1910, she started a school for girls in Kolkata, and to this day, the school is still functioning.

unlucky, in those days women were not educated. Later, I began to resent my own thoughts. What is wrong with me? Women do not read, how will I do it? Then I had a dream: I was reading the manuscript of *Chaitanya Bhagabat* (the life of a saint)... Later in the day, as I sat cooking in the kitchen, I heard my husband say to my eldest son: "Bepin, I have left my *Chaitanya Bhagabat* here. When I ask for it, bring it in." He left the book there and went away. When the book had been taken inside, I secretly took out a page and hid it carefully. It was a job hiding it, for nobody must find it in my hands. My eldest son was practising his alphabets at that time. I hid one of them as well. At times, I went over that, trying to match letters from that page with the letters that I remembered. I also tried to match the words with those that I would hear in the course of my days. With tremendous care and effort, and over a long period of time, I learnt how to read..."

After learning the alphabet, Rashsundari Devi was able to read the *Chaitanya Bhagabat*. Through her own writing she also gave the world an opportunity to read about women's lives in those days. Rashsundari Devi wrote about her everyday life experiences in details. There were days when she did not have a moment's rest, no time even to sit down and eat!

Unlike Rashsundari Devi and Rokeya Hossain, who were not allowed to learn to read and write, large numbers of girls attend school in India today. Despite this, there continue to be many girls who leave school for reasons of poverty, inadequate schooling facilities and ***discrimination****. Providing equal schooling facilities to children from all communities and class backgrounds, and particularly girls, continues to be a challenge in India.*

Schooling and education today

Today, both boys and girls attend school in large numbers. Yet, as we will see, there still remain differences between the education of boys and girls. India has a census every 10 years, which counts the whole population of the country. It also gathers detailed information about the people living in India – their age, schooling, what work they do, and so on. We use this information to measure many things, like the number of literate people, and the ratio of men and women. According to the 1961 census, about 40 per cent of all boys and men

(7 years old and above) were literate (that is, they could at least write their names) compared to just 15 per cent of all girls and women. In the most recent census of 2001, these figures have grown to 76 per cent for boys and men, and 54 per cent for girls and women. This means that the proportion of both men and women who are now able to read and have at least some amount of schooling has increased. But, as you can also see, the percentage of the male group is still higher than the female group. The gap has not gone away.

Here is a table that shows the percentage of girls and boys who leave schools from different social groups. Scheduled Caste (SC) is the official term for Dalit, and Scheduled Tribe (ST) is the official term for *Adivasi*.

School level	All boys	SC boys	ST boys	All girls	SC girls	ST girls	Total
Primary (Classes 1-5)	34	37	49	29	36	49	31
Elementary (Classes 6-8)	52	57	69	53	62	71	52
Secondary (Classes 9-10)	61	71	78	65	76	81	63

Source: Select Education Survey, GOI 2003-2004

What percentage of children leave school at the elementary level?

At which level of education do you see the highest percentage of children leaving?

Why do you think that the percentage of *Adivasi* girls and boys leaving school is higher than that of any other group?

You have probably noticed in the above table that SC and ST girls leave school at a rate that is higher than the category 'All Girls'. This means that girls who are from *Dalit* and *Adivasi* backgrounds are less likely to remain in school. The 2001 census also found that Muslim girls are less likely, than *Dalit* and *Adivasi* girls, to complete primary school. While a Muslim girl is likely to stay in school for around three years, girls from other communities spend around four years in school.

There are several reasons why children from *Dalit*, *Adivasi* and Muslim communities leave school. In many parts of the country, especially in rural and poor areas, there may not even be proper schools nor teachers who teach on a regular basis. If a school is not close to people's homes, and there is no transport like buses or vans, parents may not be willing to send their girls to school. Many families are too poor and unable to bear the cost of educating all their children. Boys may get preference in this situation. Many children also leave school because they are discriminated against by their teacher and classmates, just like Omprakash Valmiki was.

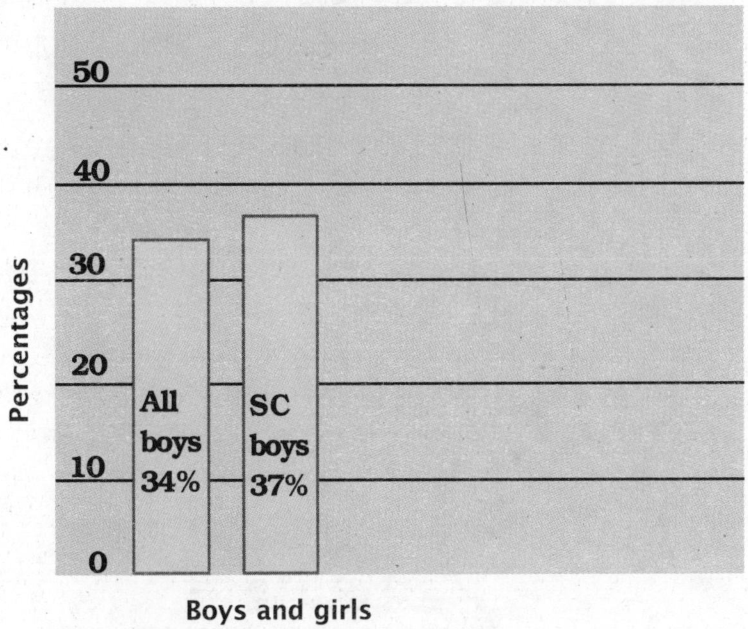

From the given table, convert the figures of primary class children who leave school into a bar diagram. The first two percentages have already been converted for you in the bar diagram on the left.

Women's movement

Women and girls now have the right to study and go to school. There are other spheres – like legal reform, violence and health – where the situation of women and girls has improved. These changes have not happened automatically. Women individually, and collectively have struggled to bring about these changes. This struggle is known as the Women's Movement. Individual women and women's organisations from different parts of the country are part of the movement. Many men support the women's movement as well. The diversity, passion and efforts of those involved makes it a very vibrant movement. Different strategies have been used to spread awareness, fight discrimination and seek justice. Here are some glimpses of this struggle.

Campaigning

Campaigns to fight discrimination and violence against women are an important part of the women's movement. Campaigns have also led to new laws being passed. A law was passed in 2006 to give women who face physical and mental violence within their homes, also called domestic violence, some legal protection.

Similarly, efforts made by the women's movement led the Supreme Court to formulate guidelines in 1997 to protect women against **sexual harassment** at the workplace and within educational institutions.

In the 1980s, for example, women's groups across the country spoke out against 'dowry deaths' — cases of young brides being murdered by their in-laws or husbands, greedy for more dowry. Women's groups spoke out against the failure to bring these cases to justice. They did so by coming on to the streets, approaching the courts, and by sharing information. Eventually, this became a public issue in the newspapers and society, and the dowry laws were changed to punish families who seek dowry.

Satyarani, an active member of the women's movement, sitting on the steps of the Supreme Court surrounded by legal files gathered during the course of a long legal battle to seek justice for her daughter who was murdered for dowry.

Raising Awareness

An important part of the women's movements' work is to raise public awareness on women's rights issues. Their message has been spread through street plays, songs and public meetings.

Protesting

The women's movement raises its voice when **violations** against women take place or for example, when a law or policy acts against their interests. Public rallies and demonstrations are a very powerful way of drawing attention to injustices.

Showing Solidarity

The women's movement is also about showing solidarity with other women and causes.

Above: Women are holding up candles to demonstrate the solidarity between the people of India and Pakistan. Every year, on 14 August, several thousand people gather at Wagah on the border of India and Pakistan and hold a cultural programme.

Below: On 8 March, International Women's Day, women all over the world come together to celebrate and renew their struggles.

EXERCISES

1. How do you think stereotypes, about what women can or cannot do, affect women's right to equality?

2. List one reason why learning the alphabet was so important to women like Rashsundari Devi, Ramabai and Rokeya.

3. "Poor girls drop out of school because they are not interested in getting an education." Re-read the last paragraph on page 62 and explain why this statement is not true.

4. Can you describe two methods of struggle that the women's movement used to raise issues? If you had to organise a struggle against stereotypes, about what women can or cannot do, what method would you employ from the ones that you have read about? Why would you choose this particular method?

Glossary

Stereotype: When we believe that people belonging to particular groups based on religion, wealth, language are bound to have certain fixed characteristics or can only do a certain type of work, we create a stereotype. For example, in this chapter, we saw how boys and girls are made to take certain subjects not because he or she has an aptitude for it, but because they are either boys or girls. Stereotypes prevent us from looking at people as unique individuals.

Discrimination: When we do not treat people equally or with respect we are indulging in discrimination. It happens when people or organisations act on their prejudices. Discrimination usually takes place when we treat some one differently or make a distinction.

Violation: When someone forcefully breaks the law or a rule or openly shows disrespect, we can say that he or she has committed a violation.

Sexual harassment: This refers to physical or verbal behaviour that is of a sexual nature and against the wishes of a woman.

UNIT FOUR

Media and Advertising

Teacher's note

Today, the media and advertising are a pervasive presence in the lives of young people, who may or may not have taken the opportunity to seriously reflect upon this fact. This Unit offers some ways by which we can begin to think about these.

The focus in 'Understanding Media' is on explaining the strong links between media and technology and media and big business. It explains how the media 'sets the agenda' through influencing our perception of issues worth devoting time and attention to, and issues that are neglected or overridden. In 'Understanding Advertising' we have focused both on critically analysing how advertising strategies influence customers, as well as demonstrating what goes into the making of an advertisement. The significance of a 'brand' and the need to promote the uniqueness of a product is a key part of advertising. The chapter identifies the mechanisms that advertisements use to appeal to the consumer, and explains how these are powerfully linked to the consumer's self-image.

Chapters 6 and 7 foreground the widespread effects of the media and advertising, and attempt to connect the issues under discussion to the learner's own lives. At the end of the media chapter, we expect the learner to recognise the role of big business in the media coverage of events — the way 'news' is selected for coverage, and the explicit/implicit dimensions of that coverage. We use two fictitious news reports to demonstrate that there is seldom just one version of a story or an event. Building on this, we expect the learner to develop the skills required to critically analyse a newspaper report or a TV story through scrutinising the information provided, as well as understanding the logic behind the exclusion of certain perspectives.

In the advertising chapter, two fictitious advertisements have been created to systematically take the learner through the techniques of crafting advertisements that appeal to the consumer. The examples focus on the significance of the key terms 'brand' and 'brand values' that are integral to advertising. These ideas can be strengthened by selecting examples from actual advertisements and structuring similar questions around them.

Both chapters conclude by linking their contents to the idea of democracy. Both emphasise, through using examples of local media as well as social advertising, how mainstream media and advertising tend to favour those who have greater financial as well as social resources. This point can be reinforced in the classroom by using local examples of media stories, as well as posing questions about the ways in which advertising is changing what is locally available as well as locally valued.

CHAPTER 6

Understanding Media

What is your favourite TV programme? What do you like listening to on the radio? Which newspaper or magazine do you usually read? Do you surf the internet and what have you found most useful about it? Did you know that there is one word that is often used to collectively refer to the radio, TV, newspapers, Internet and several other forms of communication. This word is 'media'. In this chapter, you will read more about the media. You will find out what is required to make it work, as well as the ways in which the media affects our daily lives. Can you think of one thing that you have learnt from the media this week?

Everything ranging from the stall at the local fair to the programme that you see on TV can be called media. Media is the plural form of the word 'medium' and it describes the various ways through which we communicate in society. Because media refers to all means of communication, everything ranging from a phone call to the evening news on TV can be called media. TV, radio and newspapers are a form of media that reaches millions of people, or the masses, across the country and the world and, thus, they are called mass media.

Look at the collage on the left and list six various kinds of media that you see.

Media and technology

It would probably be difficult for you to imagine your life without the media. But cable television and the widespread use of the Internet is a recent phenomenon. These have been around for less than twenty years. The technology that mass media uses keeps changing.

An artist's impression of Gutenberg printing the first sheet of the Bible.

Newspapers, television and radio can reach millions of people because they use certain technologies. We also tend to discuss newspapers and magazines as the print media; and TV and radio as the electronic media. Why do you think newspapers are called print media? As you read further, you will find that this naming is related to the different technologies that these media use. The following photographs will give you a sense of the ways in which technology that mass media uses has changed over the years and continues to change.

Ask older members of your family about what they used to listen to on the radio when there was no TV around. Find out from them when the first TV came to your area. When was cable TV introduced?

How many people in your neighbourhood use the Internet?

List three things that you know about some other part of the world from watching television?

Changing technology, or machines, and making technology more modern, helps media to reach more people. It also improves the quality of sound and the images that you see. But technology does more than this. It also changes the ways in which we think about our lives. For example, today it is quite difficult for us to think of our lives without television. Television has enabled us to think of ourselves as members of a larger global world. Television images travel huge distances through satellites and cables. This allows us to view news and entertainment channels from other parts of the world. Most of the cartoons that you see on television are mostly from Japan or the United States. We can now be sitting in Chennai or Jammu and can see images of a storm that has hit the coast of Florida in the United States. Television has brought the world closer to us.

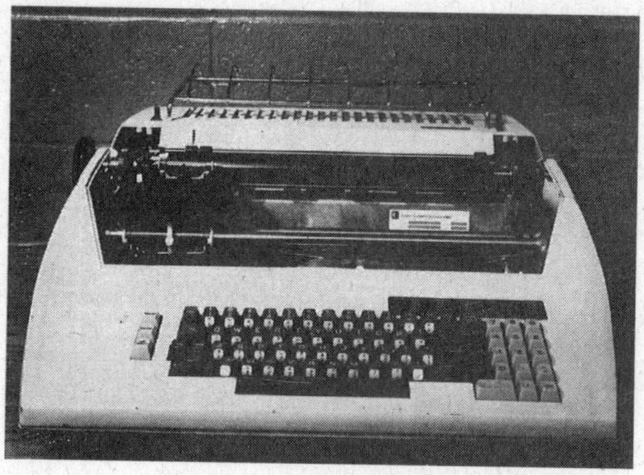

With electronic typewriters, journalism underwent a sea-change in the 1940s.

Media and money

The different technologies that mass media use are expensive. Just think about the TV studio in which the newsreader sits – it has lights, cameras, sound recorders, transmission satellites, etc., all of which cost a lot of money.

In a news studio, it is not only the newsreader who needs to be paid but also a number of other people who help put the broadcast together. This includes those who look after the cameras and lights. Also, as you read earlier the technologies that mass media use keep changing and so a lot of money is spent on getting the latest technology. Due to these costs, the mass media needs a great deal of money to do its work. As a result, most television channels and newspapers are part of big business houses.

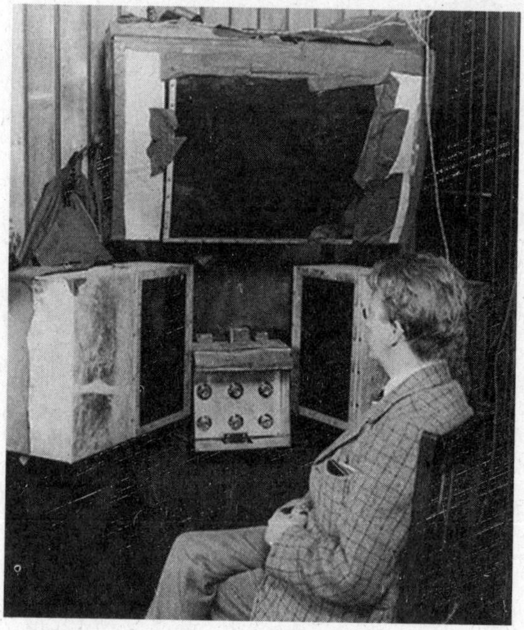

John L. Baird sits in front of the apparatus with which he demonstrated to the Royal Institute, his invention, the 'televisor', an early television.

Mass media is constantly thinking of ways to make money. One way in which the mass media earns money is by advertising different things like cars, chocolates, clothes, mobile phones, etc. You must have noticed the number of advertisements that you have to see while watching your favourite television show. While watching a cricket match on TV, the same advertisements are shown repeatedly between each over and so you are often watching the same image over and over again. As you will read in the following chapter, advertisements are repeated in the hope that you will go out and buy what is advertised.

Can you list three different products that are advertised during your favourite TV programme?

Take a newspaper and count the number of advertisements in it. Some people say that newspapers have too many advertisements. Do you think this is true and why?

Media and democracy

The cost to advertise on a news channel varies from Rs 500 to Rs 8,000 per 10 seconds depending on the popularity of the channel.

In a democracy, the media plays a very important role in providing news and discussing events taking place in the country and the world. It is on the basis of this information that citizens can, for example, learn how government works. And often, if they wish to, they can take action on the basis of these news stories. Some of the ways in which they can do this is by writing letters to the concerned minister, organising a **public protest**, starting a signature campaign, asking the government to rethink its programme, etc.

Given the role that the media plays in providing information, it is important that the information be balanced. Let us understand what we mean by a balanced media report by reading two versions of the same news event given on the next page.

News of India Report

Crackdown on polluting factories

Protestors block roads and disrupt traffic

Radhika Malik | INN

Violent protests by owners and workers brought the city to a standstill today. People getting to work could not do so on time because of huge traffic jams. The owners and workers are protesting the government's decision to close down polluting factory units. Although the government did take this decision rather hastily, the protestors have known for quite some time that their units are not legal. Moreover the levels of pollution in the city will be greatly reduced by this closure. Mr. Jain a well-known figure in the city said, "With our city gradually becoming Indias's new business hub, it is important that it be a clean and green city. Polluting factories should be moved. The factory owners and workers should accept the relocation being offered by the government instead of protesting."

India Daily Report

Closure of factories causes unre

Daily News Service ■

The closure of one lakh factories in the city's residential areas is likely to become a serious issue. On Monday, thousands of factory owners and workers took to the streets to strongly protest this closure. They said that their livelihoods would be lost. They say that the fault lies with the municipal corporation because it continued to issue licenses for new factories to be set up in residential areas.They also say that there were no adequate relocation efforts. The owners and workers plan a one-day city bandh to protest against this closure. Mr. Sharma, one of the factory owners said, "The government says that it has done a lot to relocate us. But the areas they have sent us to have no facilities and have not been developed for the last five years."

Are the above stories in the two newspapers similar? And if not, why not? What, in your view, are the similarities and the differences?

If you read the story in the *News of India*, what would you think about the issue?

The fact is that if you had read either newspaper you would only know one side of the story. If you had read the *News of India*, you would most likely think of the protestors as a nuisance. Their disrupting traffic and continually polluting the city with their factories leaves you with a bad impression about them. But on the other hand, if you had read the story in the *India Daily*, you would know that the protests are because a lot of livelihoods will be lost if the factories close because the relocation efforts have not been adequate. Neither of these stories is a balanced report. A balanced report is one that discusses all points of view of a particular story and then leaves it to the readers to make up their minds.

Writing a balanced report, however, depends on the media being independent. An independent media means that no one should control and influence its coverage of news. No one should tell the media what can be included and what should not be included in a news story. An independent media is important in a democracy. As you read above, it is on the basis of the information that the media provides that we take action as citizens, so it is important that this information is reliable and not biased.

Do you think it is important to know both sides of the story? Why?

Pretend that you are a journalist for a newspaper and write a balanced story from the two news reports.

However, the reality is that media is far from independent. This is mainly because of two reasons. The first is the control that the government has on the media. When the government prevents either a news item, or scenes from a movie, or the lyrics of a song from being shared with the larger public, this is referred to as **censorship**. There have been periods in Indian history when the government censored the media. The worst of these was the Emergency between 1975-1977.

What does TV do to us and what can we do with TV?

In many of our homes, TV is on a lot of the time. In many ways, a lot of our impressions about the world around us are formed by what we see on TV: it is like a 'window on the world'. How do you think it influences us? TV has different types of programmes, soap operas, like *Saas Bhi Kabhi Bahu Thi*, game shows, like *Kaun Banega Crorepati*, reality TV shows like *Big Boss*, news, sports and cartoons. Before, in between and after each programme are advertisements. Since TV time costs so much money, only those programmes that can attract the maximum number of viewers are shown. Can you think of what such programmes might be? Think of what are the kinds of things that TV shows and what it does not. Does it show us more about the lives of the rich or the poor?

We need to think about what TV does to us, how it shapes our views of the world, our beliefs, attitudes and values. We need to realise that it gives us a partial view of the world. While we enjoy our favourite programmes, we should always be aware of the large exciting world beyond our TV screens. There is so much happening out there that TV ignores. A world beyond film stars, celebrities and rich lifestyles, a world that all of us need to reach out to and respond to in various ways. We need to be active viewers, who question whatever we see and hear, while we may enjoy it too!

While the government does continue to censor films, it does not really censor the media's coverage of news. Despite the absence of censorship by the government, most newspapers nowadays still fail to provide a balanced story. The reasons for this are complicated. Persons who research the media have said that this happens because business houses control the media. At times, it is in the interest of these businesses to focus on only one side of the story. Media's continual need for money and its links to advertising means that it becomes difficult for media to be reporting against people who give them advertisements. Media is, thus, no longer considered independent because of its close links to business.

Besides the above, the media also tends to focus on a particular aspect of a story because they believe this makes the story interesting. Also, if they want to increase public support for an issue, they often do this by focusing on one side of a story.

Setting agendas

The media also plays an important role in deciding what stories to focus on, and therefore, decides on what is newsworthy. For example, the annual function at your school is unlikely to make the news. But if a famous actor is invited as the Chief Guest, then the media might be interested in covering it. By focusing on particular issues, the media influences our thoughts, feelings and actions, and brings those issues to our attention. Due to the significant influence it plays in our lives and in shaping our thoughts, it is commonly said that the media 'sets the agenda'.

Very recently, the media drew our attention to alarming levels of pesticides in cola drinks. They **published** reports that indicated the high level of pesticides and, thus, made us aware of the need to regularly monitor these colas according to international quality and safety standards. They did this despite the government's resistance by boldly declaring that colas were unsafe. In covering this story, the media positively helped us focus on an issue that affects our lives and one that we might not even have been aware of it had it not been for media reporting.

There are several instances when the media fails to focus on issues that are significant in our lives. For example, drinking water is a major problem in the country. Every year, thousands of people suffer and die because they do not get safe drinking water. However, we seldom find the media discussing this issue. A well-known Indian journalist wrote of how the Fashion Week, in which clothes designers show their new creations to rich people, formed the front page headlines of all the newspapers while several slums were being demolished in Mumbai, the very same week, and this was not even noticed!

As citizens of a democracy, the media has a very important role to play in our lives because it is through the media that we hear about issues related

Fashion shows are very popular with the media.

What is the consequence of the media 'setting the agenda' by reporting on the Fashion Week rather than the slum demolitions?

Can you think of an issue that does not seem important to you because it is never featured in the media?

Local media

Recognising that the media will not be interested in covering 'small' issues that involve ordinary people and their daily lives, several local groups have come forward to start their own media. Several people use community radio to tell farmers about the prices of different crops and advise them on the use of seeds and fertilisers. Others make documentary films with fairly cheap and easily available video cameras on real-life conditions faced by different poor communities, and, at times, have even given the poor these video cameras to make films on their own lives.

Another example is a newspaper called *Khabar Lahriya* which is a fortnightly that is run by eight Dalit women in Chitrakoot district in Uttar Pradesh. Written in the local language, *Bundeli*, this eight-page newspaper reports on Dalit issues and cases of violence against women and political corruption. The newspaper reaches farmers, shopkeepers, panchayat members, school teachers and women who have recently learnt to read and write.

The print media offers a large variety of information to suit the tastes of different readers.

to the working of the government. The media decides what to focus on and in this way it 'sets the agenda'. The government can, at times, prevent the media from publishing a story and this is called censorship. Nowadays, media's close relationship with business often means that a balanced report is difficult to come by. Given this, it is important for us to be aware that the 'factual information' that a news report provides is often not complete and can be one-sided. We, therefore, need to analyse the news by asking the following questions: what is the information I am learning from this report? What information is not being provided? From whose point of view is the article being written? Whose point of view is being left out and why?

EXERCISES

1. In what ways does the media play an important role in a democracy?

2. Can you give this diagram a title? What do you understand about the link between media and big business from this diagram?

3. You have read about the ways in which the media 'sets the agenda'. What kind of effect does this have in a democracy? Provide two examples to support your point of view.

4. As a class project, decide to focus on a particular news topic and cut out stories from different newspapers on this. Also watch the coverage of this topic on TV news. Compare two newspapers and write down the similarity and differences in their reports. It might help to ask the following questions-

   a. What information is this article providing?

   b. What information is it leaving out?

   c. From whose point of view is the article being written?

   d. Whose point of view is being left out and why?

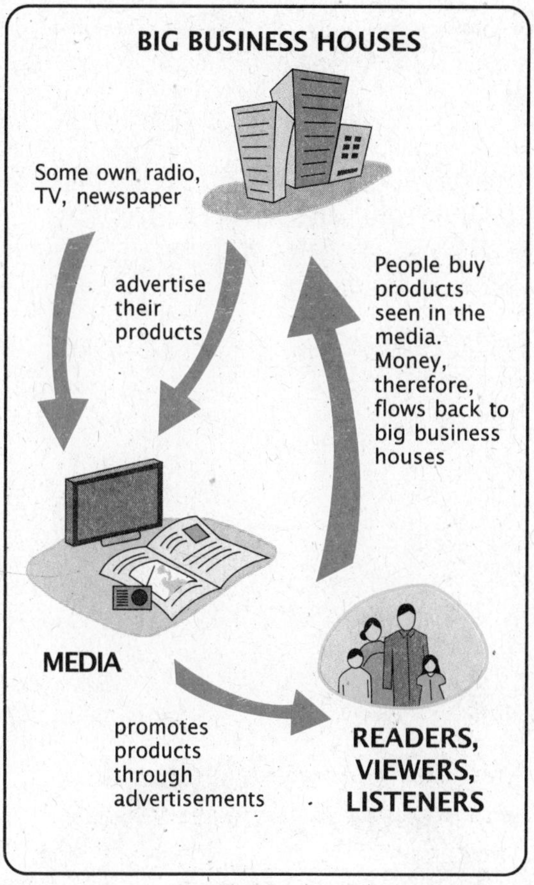
BIG BUSINESS HOUSES
Some own radio, TV, newspaper
advertise their products
People buy products seen in the media. Money, therefore, flows back to big business houses
MEDIA
promotes products through advertisements
READERS, VIEWERS, LISTENERS

Glossary

Publish: This refers to newsreports, articles, interviews, stories, etc., that are printed in newspapers, magazines and books for a wide audience to read.

Censorship: This refers to the powers that government has to disallow media from publishing or showing certain stories.

Broadcast: In this chapter this word is used to refer to a TV or radio programme that is widely transmitted.

Public protest: When a large number of people come together and openly state their opposition to some issue. Organising a rally, starting a signature campaign, blocking roads etc. are some of the ways in which this is done.

CHAPTER 7

Understanding Advertising

Today we are surrounded by advertisements or ads as we call them. We watch these on television, listen to them on radio, see them on the streets and in newspapers and magazines. Even taxis and rickshaws carry advertisements on them. When we go to cinemas, we see advertisements before the film begins and on the Internet, they often pop-up when we go into different websites. What do advertisements do? How do they attract our attention? Read more to find out...

When guests come home
give them the best
TOP TASTE DAAL

Show your child you care
Express
your love
afresh

Advertisements draw our attention to various **products** and describe them positively so that we become interested in buying them. In this chapter, we will focus on the two advertisements that you see above to understand what advertising does and how it works.

Look at the two advertisements above and fill the table.

	Top Taste Daal	Care Soap
What are the advertisements selling?		
How do they describe the product?		
What is the text trying to say?	Guests should be served this.	
What do the pictures convey?		Love of a mother.
Would you want to buy these products after seeing the advertisement?		

Building brands and brand values

Have you ever heard of the word **brand**? Advertising is all about building brands. At a very basic level, 'branding' means stamping a product with a particular name or sign. This is done in order to differentiate it from other products in the market.

So, let us look again at the advertisements above. Why do you think the manufacturers of the soap and the daal gave their products a specific name?

Do you think there is a problem in using the image of the mother as the only person who takes care of the child in the Care Soap advertisement?

Rbk

Branding actually came from cattle grazing. Cattle of different owners grazed together in ranches and they often got mixed up. The owners thought of a solution. They started marking their cattle with the owner's sign by using a heated iron. This was called 'branding'.

Daals or pulses are usually sold loose in the market. We usually know daals by their different types like masoor ki daal, urad ki daal, etc. These names are not brand names. When a company takes masoor ki daal and puts it into a packet, it will need to give the daal a special name. It needs to do this so that we don't confuse the daal in that particular packet with the daal that is sold loose. They decide on a name like 'Top Taste Daal'. This naming of the product is called 'branding'.

Similarly, in the case of the soap, there are many soaps in the market today. In bigger towns and cities, we no longer just say soap but rather refer to them using the different names of companies that make them. Given the many soaps in the market, the company will have to give the soap a different and special name. By doing this they create another brand of soap.

Just naming the product may not make us buy it. The manufacturers that made the soap and the daal still have to convince us that their soap and daal are better than the others available in the market. This is where advertising comes in. It plays a crucial role in trying to convince us to buy the product that is advertised.

Give your children great food value
Give them Best Taste Daal

The task of creating a brand does not stop at giving the product a special name. For example, just when 'Top Taste Daal' begins to be sold, another company decides to also sell daals in a packet and calls this 'Best Taste Daal'. So, now there are two branded daals in the market. Both the companies are keen that you buy their daals.

The **consumer** is confused because you really cannot tell the difference between 'Top Taste Daal' and 'Best Taste Daal'. The manufacturer has to give the consumer a reason to prefer a particular brand of daal. Just naming a daal does not help sell it. So, advertisers begin claiming certain special values for their brand. In this way, they try to differentiate it

Manufacturers spend crores of rupees to make sure that we see their advertisements wherever we go.

from other similar products. Look below at how the two daals try and do this.

From the advertisements, you can now see that the two daals are saying different things. 'Top Taste Daal' is appealing to our social tradition of treating guests extremely well. 'Best Taste Daal' is appealing to our concern for our children's health and that they eat things that are good for them. Values such as treating our guests well and making sure our children get nutritious food are used by brands to create brand values. These brand values are conveyed through the use of visuals and words to give us an overall image that appeals to us.

Brand values and social values

Advertisements are an important part of our social and cultural life today. We watch advertisements, discuss them and often judge people according to the brand products they use. Given that advertisements are such a powerful source of influence in our lives, we need to be able to understand the ways in which they work.

When guests come home
give them the best
TOP TASTE DAAL

Show your child you care
Express
your love
afresh

What does this advertisement want me to feel when I use this brand?

Who is this advertisement talking to and who is it leaving out?

If you have money to buy these products, how would you feel when you see these advertisements? If you do not have money, then how would you feel?

Let us look more closely at the two advertisements that we began the chapter with. If we ask all of the questions listed, we will realise the way in which these two advertisements work.

Branded daals cost much more than daals that are sold loose because they include the costs of packaging and advertising. So, many people cannot afford them. However, because of the advertisement, people who cannot afford Top Taste Daal might begin to feel that they are not treating their guests properly. Gradually, people will come to believe that only branded daals are good and will want to buy the daal that comes in a sealed packet rather than that which is sold loose. But, in reality there is little difference between daals that are sold loose and those sold in a packet. We are just made to imagine the difference because of the advertisement.

In the Care Soap advertisement, once again a personal emotion is being used. As a mother, if you want to show your child you care, then you have to buy this expensive soap. The advertisement uses the mother's concern for her child. It tells the mother that her love and care is best shown through using this particular brand of soap. Because of this, mothers begin to feel that using this soap is a sign of how much they love their child. In this way, the advertisement uses the love of a mother for her child to sell this expensive soap. Mothers who cannot afford this soap might begin to feel that they are not giving their children the best care.

As you can see with the two advertisements, they often target our personal emotions. By linking our personal emotions to products, advertisements tend to influence the ways in which we value ourselves as persons.

Often several of our cricket heroes and our favourite film stars also try and sell products to us through advertisements. We may feel tempted to buy these products because persons whom we consider our heroes tell us that they are worth buying. In addition, advertisements often show us images of the **lifestyles** of rich people and seldom show us the reality of peoples' lives that we see around us.

This collage, prepared by school children, shows celebrities promoting products. It was recently reported that a top cricketer signed a three-year contract to do various advertisements for Rs 180 crores. A popular model may charge Rs 5 lakh or more per advertisement.

Advertisements play a big role in our lives. We not only buy products based on them, but often, having certain brand products influences the ways in which we think about ourselves, our friends and our family. It is, therefore, important to know how advertising works and understand what it does before we choose to buy the products that advertisements sell. We need to be able to critically understand why they use particular images, the personal emotion that they are appealing to and the ways in which this affects how we think about ourselves when we use the product or are not able to buy it.

The telecast rate for a 30 second advertisement on a major TV channel is Rs 1.65 lakh. The cost of bringing out a quarter page colour advertisement in a leading newspaper is Rs 8.36 lakh.

How does an advertisement get made?

Advertising is a very important part of getting people to buy a brand. This does not happen easily and several hundred books have been written on this. Advertisements aim to get people to buy a particular brand. This basically means that after we see an advertisement we should *want* to buy the brand. Let us see how the persons who make advertisements decide on what images, text and personal emotions to use to sell the product.

THE LOVING SOAP

At the office of a prominent advertising agency...

A couple of weeks later...

The creative team at the agency starts thinking...

All the existing brands of baby soap in the market emphasise 'naturalness', etc. We need a different angle.
How about associating our soap with the loving care of the mother! We should say that you cannot fully express your love for your child without your soap!
EXPRESSION
We need a good brand name to go with that.
How about Care Soap?
Yes, that's a brilliant idea!

The agency makes a presentation to the client...

Our campaign will be based on the concept: 'Care Soap – Express Your Love Afresh'. The visuals will focus on mothers and children to re-inforce our brand strategy!
care
care
I like the concept!

The visuals and advertisements are then tested amongst the target audience.

Yes. I think this promotes a new way of expressing love and care. I would like to try this new brand.
SALE
Thank you Madam!

Once the marketing strategy is considered successful, the advertisement campaign is finalised and released in various media along with the launch of the new care soap.

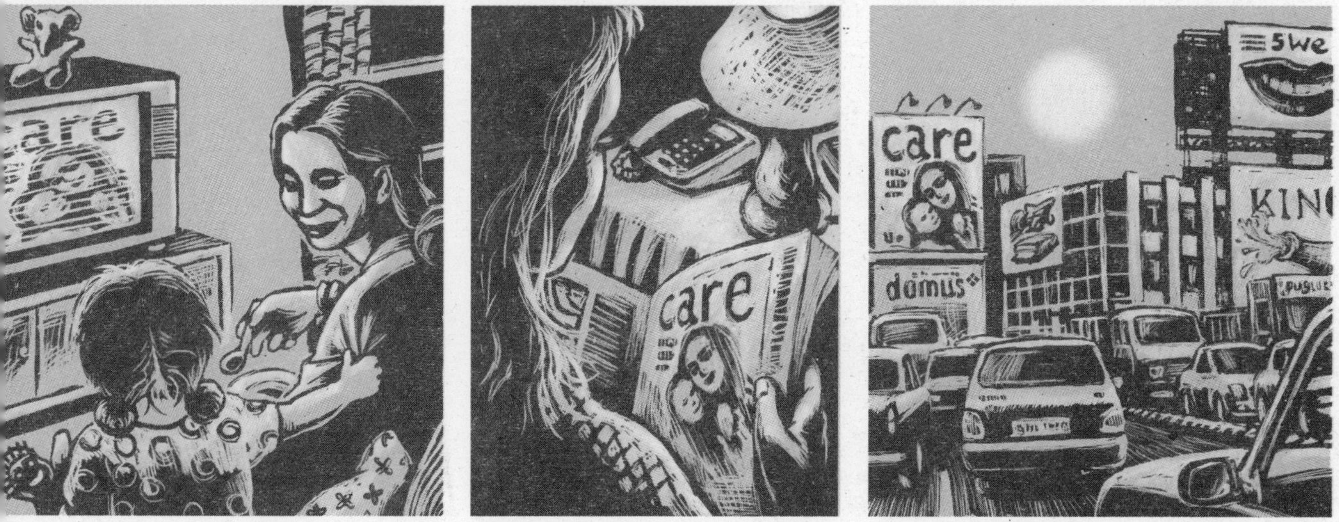

Advertising and democracy

There are various ways in which advertising links to issues of equality in a democratic society.

Advertising a product costs a lot of money. Usually, crores of rupees are spent advertising a brand. Producing and showing advertisements in the media is very expensive. Because there are so many advertisements in the market today, companies have to show the advertisement again and again to have it stick in people's minds.

What this often means is that only large companies can advertise. If you own a small business, you will not have the money to show your product on TV or national newspapers and magazines. So, persons who sell papad, pickles, sweets and jams that they have made at home are not considered as fashionable as brand products. They often have to sell their

Who do you think is the target audience for the social advertisements below?

What is the message that each social advertisement is trying to get across?

Having read about diarhhoea epidemic in the chapter on State Government, can you make a social advertisement on what precautionary steps should be taken to prevent diarrhoea?

Social advertising

Social advertisements refer to advertisements made by the State or private agencies that have a larger message for society. The following are two social advertisements:

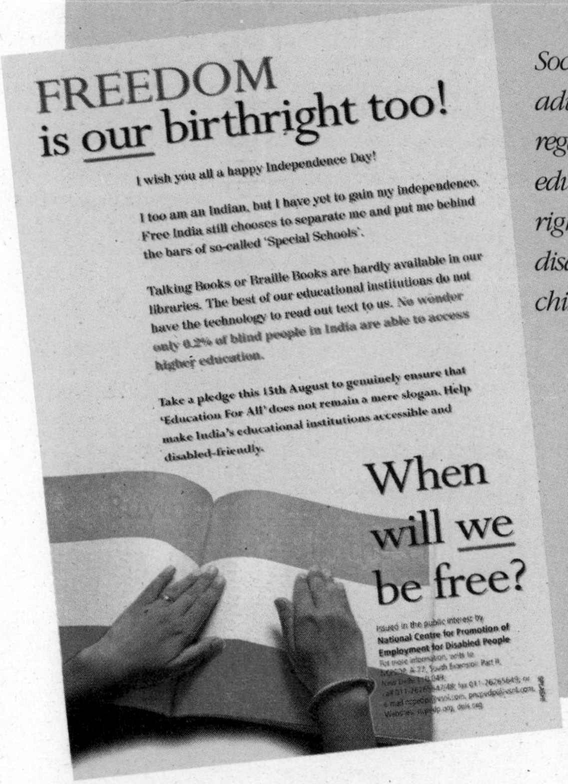

Social advertisement regarding educational rights of disabled children.

Social advertisement regarding crossing of unmanned railway crossings.

products in weekly markets and neighbourhood shops that you will read about in the following unit.

It also makes us believe that things that are packaged and have a brand name are far better than things that do not come in packets. We forget that the quality of a product has little to do with the packaging that it comes in. This shift to packaged products negatively affects the sales of several small businesses forcing people out of their livelihoods.

Advertising makes us believe that things that are packaged are better than things that do not come in packets.

In a democracy in which all people are equal and should be able to lead a life of dignity, advertising tends to promote a certain lack of respect for the poor. They are not the faces we most often see in advertisements and so we tend to dismiss their lives as worthless.

Advertising, because it appeals to personal emotions also tends to make people who cannot afford certain brands feel bad. They feel that they are unable to give their loved ones the best care that brand products appear to offer.

Juice sellers like this one are losing customers who, because of advertising, prefer branded drinks.

Advertising by focusing on the lives of the rich and famous helps us forget about issues of poverty, discrimination and dignity, all of which are central to the functioning of equality in a democracy. More than just selling us products, advertisements tell us how we should live our lives, what we should aspire and dream for, how we should express our love, what it means to be smart, successful and beautiful. As citizens of a democratic society, it is important for us to be aware of the strong influence that advertising has on our lives. By critically understanding what advertisements do, we can make better decisions about whether we wish to buy a product or not.

EXERCISES

1. What do you understand by the word brand? List two reasons why building brands is central to advertising?

2. Choose two of your favourite print advertisements. Now, look at each of these and answer the following questions:

   a. What visuals and text is being used in these advertisements to attract my attention?

   b. What values are being promoted in these advertisements?

   c. Who is this advertisement speaking to and who is it leaving out?

   d. If you could not afford the brand that is being advertised how would you feel?

3. Can you explain two ways in which you think advertising affects issues of equality in a democracy?

4. Making an advertisement requires a lot of creativity. Let us imagine a situation in which a manufacturer has just made a new watch. She says that she wants to sell this watch to school children. She comes to your class and asks you all to create a brand name as well as an advertisement for the watch. Divide the class into small groups and each group create an advertisement for this watch. Share it with the class.

Glossary

Product: This refers to a thing or service that has been made for being sold in the market.

Consumer: This refers to the person for whom the goods or products have been made and who pays money to buy and use them.

Brand: This refers to a special identification or name that is associated with a product. Such identification is created through the process of advertising.

To influence: This refers to the power to change what someone believes or does.

Lifestyle: In this chapter, this word refers to people's lives being identified by the products they own, the clothes they wear, the places they eat in, etc.

UNIT FIVE

Markets

Teacher's note

These two chapters focus on aspects of life and commercial cycles associated with markets. While some of these processes may be visible and, therefore, easily observable, there are also others that are relatively unfamiliar.

Chapter 8 discusses 'Markets Around Us'. At one level, we study different market sites: a weekly market, neighbourhood shops, a shopping complex, etc. At another level, we explore the intricate question, 'how do goods reach these markets?' We examine how a chain of markets operates and the role of wholesale markets within this, through the case study of a wholesale vegetable market. We usually associate 'market' with marketplaces, but buying and selling takes place in diverse ways and the chapter discusses how all of this falls within a larger understanding of markets.

Chapter 9 looks at how markets offer people different opportunities. This is done through the 'story of a shirt', and the chain of markets involved in the process. Together with understanding each step of the manufacture and circulation of a shirt, we realise that some people stand to gain in the market transaction whereas others do not gain as much, or none at all. The opportunities are highly unequal. Ways do exist, such as those of cooperative marketing, which can provide a better return to the producers. However, we need to find many more viable avenues for equitable distribution.

These chapters offer an opportunity of bringing in the experience of local markets for discussion in the classroom. A visit to a wholesale market would be of interest, and would allow the learner to find out the profit margins and details of daily earnings so that those inequalities can be directly examined. The experiences of markets are varied and also quite rich. Hence, one should allocate time for some questions, not addressed in the text, which students may wish to discuss.

CHAPTER 8

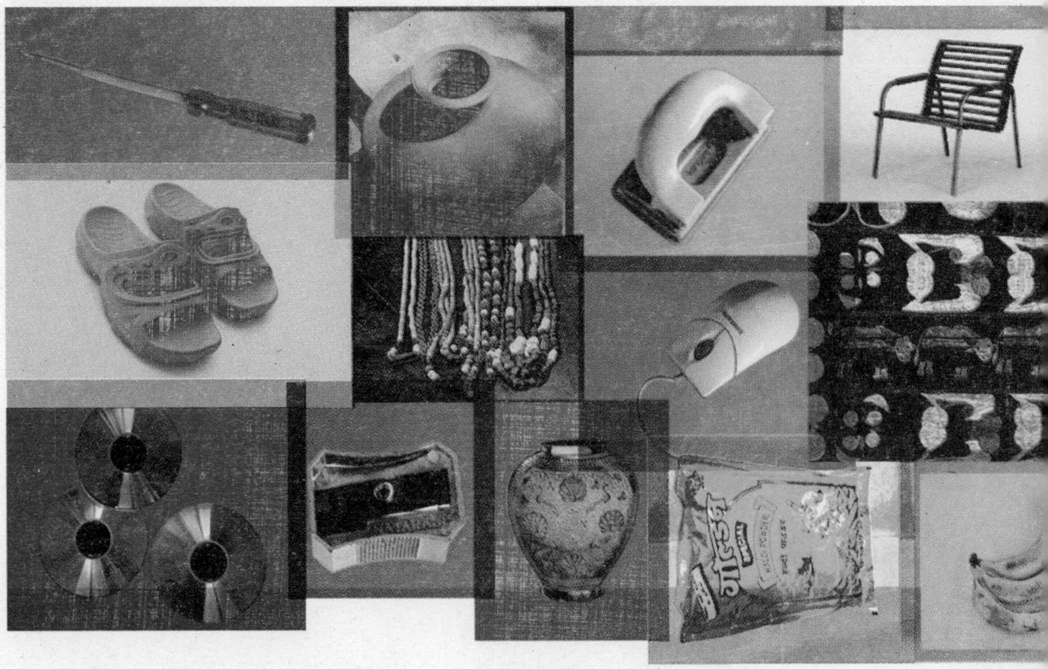

Markets Around Us

We go to the market to buy many things – vegetables, soap, toothpaste, masala, bread, rice, dal, clothes, notebooks, biscuits, etc. If we make a list of the goods that we purchase, it would be really long. There are many kinds of markets that we may visit for our everyday needs: these can include shops, hawker's stalls in our neighbourhood, a weekly market, a large shopping complex, perhaps even a mall. In this chapter, we look at some of these markets and try to understand how the goods that are sold there reach buyers, who these buyers are, who these sellers are, and the sorts of problems they face.

AA batteries
edicines for Nani
Photocopies
Sketch pens
5. Gift for Kav
6. Diwali Cards
7. Chappal
1 kg Rice
1/2 kg Masoor
~~1/2 kg Sugar~~
100 gm. Butter
Washing bar
Toothpaste
1 doz. clothes pegs
5m. Nylon
CLEANERS &
PISTA
CHOCOL
QALA-QA
GULAB-JA
RABRI
RAS-MALA
RASGULLEY

Why do people go to a weekly market? Give three reasons.

Who are the sellers in a weekly market? Why don't we find big business persons in these markets?

Why are things cheap in the weekly market?

Explain with an example how people bargain in the market. Can you think of a situation where the bargain would be unfair?

Sameer: Seller of clothes

Sameer is a small trader in the weekly market. He buys clothes from a large trader in the town and sells them in six different markets in a week. He and other cloth sellers move in groups. They hire a mini van for this. His customers are from villages that are near the marketplace. At festival times, such as during Deepavali or Pongal, he does good business.

Weekly market

A weekly market is so called because it is held on a specific day of the week. Weekly markets do not have permanent shops. Traders set up shops for the day and then close them up in the evening. Then they may set up at a different place the next day. There are thousands of such markets in India. People come here for their everyday requirements.

Many things in weekly markets are available at cheaper rates. This is because when shops are in permanent buildings, they incur a lot of expenditure – they have to pay rent, electricity, fees to the government. They also have to pay wages to their workers. In weekly markets, these shop owners store the things they sell at home. Most of them are helped by their family members and, hence, do not need to hire workers. Weekly markets also have a large number of shops selling the same goods which means there is competition among them. If some trader were to charge a high price, people would move to another shop where the same thing may be available more cheaply or where the buyer can bargain and bring the price down.

One of the advantages of weekly markets is that most things you need are available at one place. Whether you want vegetables, groceries or cloth items, utensils – all of them can be found here. You do not have to go to different areas to buy different things. People also prefer going to a market where they have a choice and a variety of goods.

Shops in the neighbourhood

We have seen that the weekly markets offer a variety of goods. However, we also buy things from other kinds of markets. There are many shops that sell goods and services in our neighbourhoods. We may buy milk from the dairy, groceries from departmental stores, stationery, eatables or medicines from other

Sujata and Kavita were sent to buy groceries from their neighbourhood shop. This was the shop they usually went to. It was crowded today. The shop owner managed the shop herself with two helpers. When they managed to get into the shop, Sujata dictated a list to her. She in turn began asking her helpers to weigh and pack the items. Meanwhile Kavita looked around...

On the top left shelf there were different brands of detergent cakes. Another shelf had toothpastes, talcum powder, shampoo, hair oil. The different brands and different colours looked so attractive. On the floor lay a few sacks.

It took almost 20 minutes to weigh and pack all the groceries. Then Sujata showed her "notebook." The woman noted the amount of Rs.1550 in the notebook and gave it back. She also noted the amount in her big register. Then Sujata took the heavy bags out of the shop. Her family will pay for the purchases in the first week of next month.

shops. Many of these are permanent shops, while others are roadside stalls such as that of the vegetable hawker, the fruit vendor, the mechanic, etc.

Shops in the neighbourhood are useful in many ways. They are near our home and we can go there on any day of the week. Usually, the buyer and seller know each other and these shops also provide goods on credit. This means that you can pay for the purchases later, as we saw in Sujata's case, for example.

Why did Sujata carry a notebook? Do you think this system is useful? Can there be problems?

What are the different kinds of shops that you find in your neighbourhood? What do you purchase from them?

Why are goods sold in permanent shops costlier than those sold in the weekly markets or by roadside hawkers?

You might have noticed that there are different kinds of sellers even in the neighbourhood markets. Some of them have permanent shops and others sell their goods on the roadside.

Anzal Mall is a five-floor shopping complex. Kavita and Sujata were enjoying going up and down in the lift. It seemed as if it was made of glass and they were able to see outside as they went up. It was fascinating to see so many different kinds of shops such as the ice-cream, burger, pizza and other food shops; shops full of home appliances; footwear and leather items as well as bookshops.

While wandering about on the third floor they entered a shop that was selling branded ready-made clothes. The security guard looked at them as if he wanted to stop them but he did not say anything. They looked at some dresses and then looked at the price tag. None of them was less than Rs 2,000, almost five times the weekly market price! Sujata whispered to Kavita, "I'll take you to another shop which has good quality ready-made clothes at more reasonable prices".

Why do you think the guard wanted to stop Kavita and Sujata from entering the shop? What would you say if someone stops you from entering a shop in a market?

Shopping complexes and malls

So far we have seen two kinds of marketplaces – weekly markets and markets in our neighbourhood. There are other markets in the urban area that have many shops, popularly called shopping complexes. These days, in many urban areas, you also have large multi-storeyed air-conditioned buildings with shops on different floors, known as malls. In these urban markets, you get both branded and non-branded goods. As you have read in the chapter on advertising, branded goods are expensive, often promoted by advertising and claims of better quality. The companies producing these products sell them through shops in large urban markets and, at times, through special showrooms. As compared to non-branded goods, fewer people can afford to buy branded ones.

Why do people not bargain in shops located in malls whereas they bargain in weekly markets?

Chain of markets

In the previous sections, you have read about different markets from where we buy goods. From where do you think shop-owners procure their goods? Goods are produced in factories, on farms and in homes. However, we don't buy directly from the factory or from the farm. Nor would the producers be interested in selling us small quantities such as one kilo of vegetables or one plastic mug.

How do you think your neighbourhood shop gets its goods? Find out and explain with some examples.

Why is a wholesale trader necessary?

The people in between the producer and the final consumer are the traders. The wholesale trader first buys goods in large quantities. For example, the vegetable wholesale trader will not buy a few kilos of vegetables, but will buy in large lots of 25 to 100 kilos. These will then be sold to other traders. In these markets, buying and selling takes place between traders. It is through these links of traders that goods reach faraway places. The trader who finally sells this to the consumer, is the retailer. This could be a trader in a weekly market, a hawker in the neighbourhood or a shop in a shopping complex.

We can understand this with the help of the following examples –

Every city has areas for wholesale markets. This is where goods first reach and are then supplied to other traders. The roadside hawker whom you read about earlier would have purchased a large quantity of plastic items from a wholesale trader in the town. He, in turn, might have bought these from another, even bigger wholesale trader in the city. The city

The above map of Delhi shows four of the 10 wholesale markets in the city.

wholesale trader would have bought a large quantity of plastic items from the factory and stored them in a godown. In this way, a chain of markets is set up. When we purchase, we may not be aware of the chain of markets through which these goods travel before they reach us.

Aftab – The wholesaler in the city

Aftab is one of the wholesale traders who purchases in bulk. His business starts around 2 o'clock in the morning when vegetables reach the market. This is the time when the vegetable market or mandi starts buzzing with activity. The vegetables come in trucks, matadors, tractor trolleys from farms both near and far. Soon the process of auctions begins. Aftab participates in this auction and decides what he will buy. Today, for example, he bought 5 quintals of cauliflower, 10 quintals of onions. He has a shop in the market where he stores the vegetables that he has bought. From here he sells to hawkers and shopkeepers who start coming to the market around six in the morning. They have to organise their purchases so that they can start their shop for the day around ten in the morning.

Markets everywhere

So far we have seen different marketplaces where people buy and sell a variety of goods and services. All these markets are in a specific locality and work in a particular manner and time. However, it is not always necessary that one has to go to the market to purchase goods. You can place orders for a variety of things through the phone and these days through the Internet, and the goods are delivered at your home. In clinics and nursing homes, you may have noticed sales representatives waiting for doctors. Such persons are also engaged in the selling of goods. Thus, buying and selling takes place in different ways, not necessarily through shops in the market.

The markets that we looked at above are the ones that we recognise easily. However, there are markets that we may not be so aware of. This is because a

People in urban areas can enter markets without stepping out of their homes via the Internet. They use their credit cards to make 'online purchases'.

large number of goods are bought and sold that we don't use directly. For example, a farmer uses fertilisers to grow crops that he purchases from special shops in the city and they, in turn get them from factories. A car factory purchases engine, gears, petrol tanks, axles, wheels, etc. from various other factories. We don't usually see all the buying and selling, but only the final product – the car in the showroom. The story is similar for any other good.

Markets and equality

In this chapter, we have looked at shop owners in a weekly market and those in a shopping complex. They are very different people. One is a small trader with little money to run the shop whereas the other is able to spend a lot of money to set up the shop. They also earn unequal amounts. The weekly market trader earns little compared to the profit of a regular shop owner in a shopping complex. Similarly, buyers are differently placed. There are many who are not able to afford the cheapest of goods while others are busy shopping in malls. Thus, whether we can be buyers or sellers in these different markets depends, among other things, on the money that we have.

A car being put together in a factory.

We have also examined the chain of markets that is formed before goods can reach us. It is through

Malls, like the one above, sell expensive and branded goods.

this chain that what is produced in one place reaches people everywhere. When things are sold, it encourages production and new opportunities are created for people to earn. However, do they offer equal opportunities? We will try to understand this through the story of a shirt in the next chapter.

EXERCISES

1. In what ways is a hawker different from a shop owner?
2. Compare and contrast a weekly market and a shopping complex on the following:

Market	Kind of goods sold	Prices of goods	Sellers	Buyers
Weekly market				
Shopping complex				

3. Explain how a chain of markets is formed. What purpose does it serve?
4. 'All persons have equal rights to visit any shop in a marketplace.' Do you think this is true of shops with expensive products? Explain with examples.
5. 'Buying and selling can take place without going to a marketplace.' Explain this statement with the help of examples.

Glossary

Weekly market: These markets are not daily markets but are to be found at a particular place on one or maybe two days of the week. These markets most often sell everything that a household needs ranging from vegetables to clothes to utensils.

Mall: This is an enclosed shopping space. This is usually a large building with many floors that has shops, restaurants and, at times, even a cinema theatre. These shops most often sell branded products.

Wholesale: This refers to buying and selling in large quantities. Most products, including vegetables, fruits and flowers have special wholesale markets.

Chain of markets: A series of markets that are connected like links in a chain because products pass from one market to another.

CHAPTER 9

A Shirt in the Market

This chapter tells us the story of a shirt ! It begins with the production of cotton and ends with the sale of the shirt. We shall see that a chain of markets links the producer of cotton to the buyer of the shirt in the supermarket. Buying and selling takes place at every step in the chain. Does everyone benefit equally from this? Or do some people benefit more than others? We shall find out.

A cotton farmer in Kurnool

Swapna, a small farmer in Kurnool (Andhra Pradesh) grows cotton on her small piece of land. The bolls of the cotton plant are ripe and some have already burst, so Swapna is busy picking cotton. The bolls, which carry the cotton in them, do not burst open all at once so it takes several days to harvest the cotton.

Once the cotton is collected, instead of selling it at Kurnool cotton market, Swapna and her husband take the harvest to the local trader. At the beginning of the cropping season, Swapna had borrowed Rs 2,500 from the trader at a very high interest rate to buy seeds, fertilisers, pesticides for cultivation. At that time, the local trader made Swapna agree to another condition. He made her promise to sell all her cotton to him.

Cultivation of cotton requires high levels of inputs such as fertilisers and pesticides and the farmers have to incur heavy expenses on account of these. Most often, the small farmers need to borrow money to meet these expenses.

At the trader's yard, two of his men weigh the bags of cotton. At a price of Rs 1,500 per quintal, the cotton fetches Rs 6,000. The trader deducts Rs 3,000 for repayment of loan and interest and pays Swapna Rs 3,000.

Swapna: Rs 3,000 only!

Trader: Cotton is selling cheap. There is a lot of cotton in the market.

Swapna: I have toiled so hard for four months to grow this cotton. You can see how fine and clean the cotton is this time. I had hoped to get a much better price.

Did Swapna get a fair price on the cotton?

Why did the trader pay Swapna a low price?

Where do you think large farmers would sell their cotton? How is their situation different from Swapna?

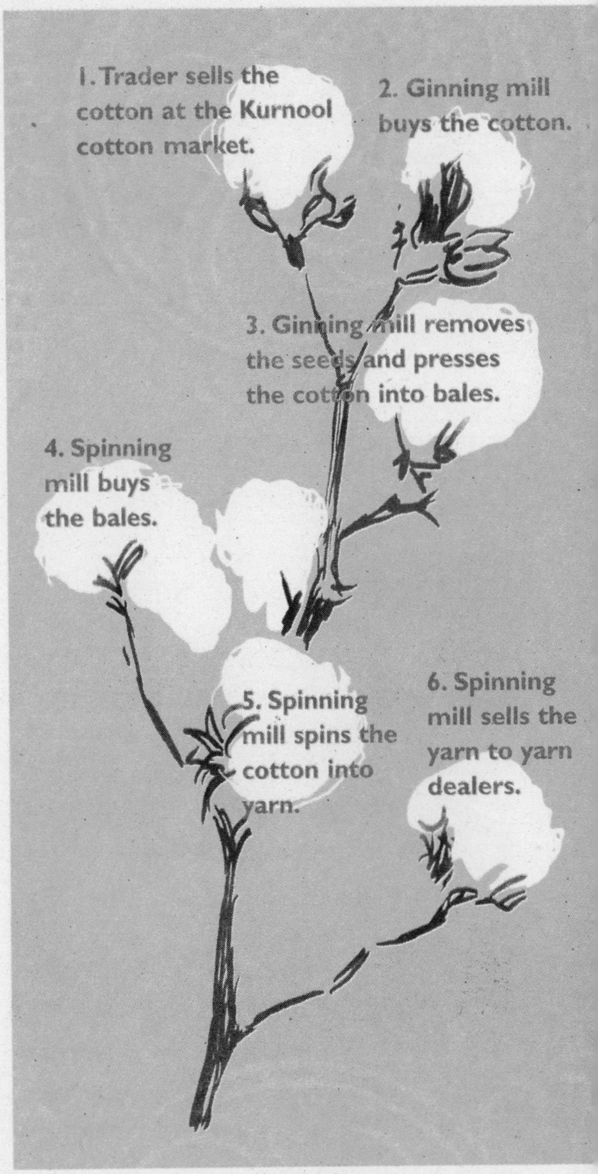

1. Trader sells the cotton at the Kurnool cotton market.
2. Ginning mill buys the cotton.
3. Ginning mill removes the seeds and presses the cotton into bales.
4. Spinning mill buys the bales.
5. Spinning mill spins the cotton into yarn.
6. Spinning mill sells the yarn to yarn dealers.

Trader: Amma, I am giving you a good price. Other traders are not even paying this much. You can check at the Kurnool market, if you do not believe me.

Swapna: Don't be angry. How can I doubt you? I had only hoped that we would earn enough from the cotton crop to last us a few months.

Though Swapna knows that cotton will sell for at least Rs 1,800 per quintal, she doesn't argue further. The trader is a powerful man in the village and the farmers have to depend on him for loans not only for cultivation, but also to meet other exigencies such as illnesses, children's school fees. Also, there are times in the year when there is no work and no income for the farmers, so borrowing money is the only means of survival.

Swapna's earning from cotton cultivation is barely more than what she might have earned as a wage labourer.

The cloth market of Erode

Erode's bi-weekly cloth market in Tamil Nadu is one of the largest cloth markets in the world. A large variety of cloth is sold in this market. Cloth that is made by weavers in the villages around is also brought here for sale. Around the market are offices of cloth merchants who buy this cloth. Other traders from many south Indian towns also come and purchase cloth in this market.

A shop in Erode.

On market days, you would also find weavers bringing cloth that has been made on order from the merchant. These merchants supply cloth on order to garment manufacturers and exporters around the country. They purchase the yarn and give instructions to the weavers about the kind of cloth that is to be made. In the following example, we can see how this is done.

1.This is a merchant's shop in the bazaar. Over the years, these traders have developed extensive contacts with garment firms around the country from whom they get orders. These traders purchase the yarn (thread) from others.
2. The weavers live in villages around and take the yarn supplied by these traders to their homes where the looms are located in sheds adjacent to their houses. This photograph shows a powerloom in one such home.
The weavers and their families spend long hours working on these looms. Most weaving units have about 2–8 powerlooms on which the yarn is woven into cloth. A variety of sarees, towels, shirting, ladies dress material and bedsheets are produced in these looms.
3. They then bring back the finished cloth to the traders. Here, they can be seen getting ready to go to the merchant in the town. The trader keeps an account of the yarn given and pays them money for weaving this into cloth.

Putting-out system–weavers producing cloth at home

The merchant distributes work among the weavers based on the orders he has received for cloth. The weavers get the yarn from the merchant and supply him the cloth. For the weavers, this arrangement seemingly has two advantages. The weavers do not have to spend their money on purchase of yarn. Also, the problem of selling the finished cloth is taken care of. Weavers know from the outset what cloth they should make and how much of it is to be woven.

However, this dependence on the merchants both for raw materials and markets means that the merchants have a lot of power. They give orders for what is to be made and they pay a very low price for making the cloth. The weavers have no way of

What are the following people doing at the Erode cloth market–merchants, weavers, exporters?

In what ways are weavers dependent on cloth merchants?

If the weavers were to buy yarn on their own and sell cloth, they would probably earn three times more. Do you think this is possible? How? Discuss.

Do you find similar 'putting-out' arrangements in making *papads, masalas, beedis*? Find out about this in your area and discuss in class.

You might have heard of cooperatives in your area. It could be in milk, provisions, paddy, etc. Find out for whose benefit they were set up?

knowing who they are making the cloth for or at what price it will be sold. At the cloth market, the merchants sell the cloth to the garment factories. In this way, the market works more in favour of the merchants.

Weavers invest all their savings or borrow money at high interest rates to buy looms. Each loom costs Rs 20,000, so a small weaver with two looms has to invest Rs 40,000. The work on these looms cannot be done alone. The weaver and another adult member of his family work upto 12 hours a day to produce cloth. For all this work, they earn about Rs 3,500 per month.

The arrangement between the merchant and the weavers is an example of **putting-out system,** whereby the merchant supplies the raw material and receives the finished product. It is prevalent in the weaving industry in most regions of India.

Weaver's cooperative

We have seen that the weavers are paid very little by the merchant under the putting out system. Weaver's cooperatives are one way to reduce the dependence on the merchant and to earn a higher income for the weavers. In a cooperative, people with common interests come together and work for their mutual benefit. In a weaver's cooperative, the weavers form a group and take up certain activities collectively. They procure yarn from the yarn dealer and distribute it among the weavers. The cooperative also does the marketing. So, the role of the merchant is reduced, and weavers get a fair price on the cloth.

At times, the government helps the cooperatives by buying cloth from them at a reasonable price. For instance, the Tamil Nadu government runs a Free School Uniform programme in the state. The government procures the cloth for this programme from the powerloom weaver's cooperatives. Similarly, the government buys cloth from the handloom weaver's cooperatives and sells it through stores known as Co-optex. You might have come across one of these stores in your town.

Women workers sewing buttons in a garment factory.

The garment exporting factory near Delhi

The Erode merchant supplies the cotton cloth produced by the weavers to a garment exporting factory near Delhi. The garment exporting factory will use the cloth to make shirts. The shirts will be exported to foreign buyers. Among the foreign buyers are businesspersons from the US and Europe who run a chain of stores. These large stores do business strictly on their own terms. They demand the lowest prices from the supplier. In addition, they set high standards for quality of production and timely delivery. Any defects or delay in delivery is dealt with strictly. So, the **exporter** tries his best to meet the conditions set by these powerful buyers.

What are the demands foreign buyers make on the garment exporters? Why do the garment exporters agree to these demands?

Faced with such pressures from the buyers, the garment exporting factories, in turn, try to cut costs. They get the maximum work out of the workers at the lowest possible wages. This way they can maximise their own profits and also supply the garments to foreign buyers at a cheap price.

How do the garment exporters meet the conditions set by the foreign buyers?

Why do you think more women are employed in the Impex garment factory? Discuss.

The Impex garment factory has 70 workers. Most of them are women. Most of these workers are employed on a temporary basis. This means that whenever the employer feels that a worker is not needed, the worker can be asked to leave. Workers' wages are fixed according to their skills. The highest paid among the workers are the tailors who get about Rs 3,000 per month. Women are employed as helpers for thread cutting, buttoning, ironing and packaging. These jobs have the lowest wages.

Write a letter to the Minister asking for what you think would be proper payment to the workers.

Payment to workers (per month)

Tailoring	Rs 3,000
Ironing	Rs 1.50 (per piece)
Checking	Rs 2,000
Thread cutting and buttoning	Rs 1,500

The shirt below shows the profit made by the businessperson, and the various costs that he had to pay. Find out from the diagram below, what the cost price includes.

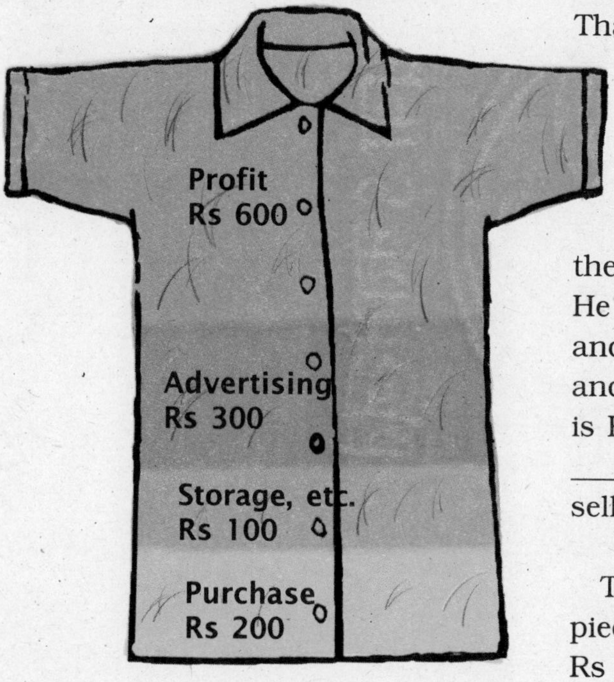

The shirt in the United States

A number of shirts are on display at a large clothes shop in the United States, and are priced at $26. That is, each shirt sells for $26 or around Rs 1,200.

Use the diagram shown in the margin to fill in the blanks below.

The businessperson purchased the shirts from the garment exporter in Delhi for Rs _______ per shirt. He then spent Rs _______ for advertising in the media, and another Rs _______ per shirt on storage, display and all other charges. Thus, the cost to this person is Rs 600 while he sells the shirt for Rs 1,200. Rs _________ is his profit on one shirt! If he is able to sell a large number of shirts, his profit will be higher.

The garment exporter sold the shirt at Rs 200 per piece. The cloth and other raw materials cost him Rs 70 per shirt. The workers' wages cost another

Rs 15 per shirt. The cost of running his office came to Rs 15 per shirt. Can you calculate the profit per shirt for the garment exporter?

Who are the gainers in the market?

A chain of markets links the producer of cotton to the buyer at the supermarket. Buying and selling takes place at every step in the chain. Let us recall who were the people who were involved in this process of buying and selling. Did they all gain as much? There were people who made profits in the market and there were some who did not gain as much from this buying and selling. Despite their having toiled very hard, they earned little. Can you place them in the table shown here?

Market and equality

The foreign businessperson made huge **profits** in the market. Compared to this, the garment exporter made only moderate profits. On the other hand, the earnings of the workers at the garment export factory are barely enough to cover their day-to-day needs. Similarly, we saw the small cotton farmer and the weaver at Erode put in long hours of hard work. But they did not get a fair price in the market for what they produced. The merchants or traders are somewhere in between. Compared to the weavers, they have earned more but it is still much less than the exporter. Thus, not everyone gains equally in the market. Democracy is also about getting a fair wage in the market. Whether it is Kanta or Swapna, if families don't earn enough how would they think of themselves as equal to others?

On one hand, the market offers people opportunities for work and to be able to sell things that they grow or produce. It could be the farmer selling cotton or the weaver producing cloth. On the other hand, it is usually the rich and the powerful

Compare the earnings per shirt of the worker in the garment factory, the garment exporter and the businessperson in the market abroad. What do you find?

What are the reasons that the businessperson is able to make a huge profit in the market?

You have read the chapter on advertising. Why does the businessperson spend Rs 300 per shirt on advertising? Discuss.

People who gained in the market
1. ____________
2. ____________
3. ____________
People who didn't gain as much in the market
1. ____________
2. ____________
3. ____________

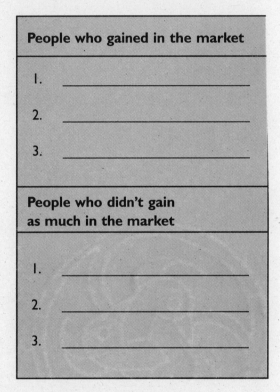

Did you know that the readymade clothes that you buy require the work of so many different persons?

that get the maximum earnings from the market. These are the people who have money and own the factories, the large shops, large land holdings, etc. The poor have to depend on the rich and the powerful for various things. They have to depend for loans (as in the case of Swapna, the small farmer), for raw materials and marketing of their goods (weavers in the putting-out system), and most often for employment (workers at the garment factory). Because of this dependence, the poor are exploited in the market. There are ways to overcome these such as forming cooperatives of producers and ensuring that laws are followed strictly. In the last chapter, we will read about how one such fish-workers' cooperative was started on the Tawa river.

EXERCISES

1. What made Swapna sell the cotton to the trader instead of selling at the Kurnool cotton market?

2. Describe the conditions of employment as well as the wages of workers in the garment exporting factory. Do you think the workers get a fair deal?

3. Think of something common that we use. It could be sugar, tea, milk, pen, paper, pencil, etc. Discuss through what chain of markets this reaches you. Can you think of the people that help in the production or trade?

4. Arrange the statements given alongside in the correct order and then fill in the numbers in the cotton bolls accordingly. The first two have already been done for you.

1. Swapna sells the cotton to the trader.
2. Customers buy these shirts in a supermarket.
3. Trader sells cotton to the Ginning Mill.
4. Garment exporters buy the cloth from merchants for making shirts.
5. Yarn dealers or merchants give the yarn to the weavers.
6. The exporter sells shirts to the businessperson from the USA.
7. Spinning mill buys the cotton and sells yarn to the yarn dealers.
8. Weavers return with the cloth.
9. Ginning mill cleans the cotton and makes it into bales.

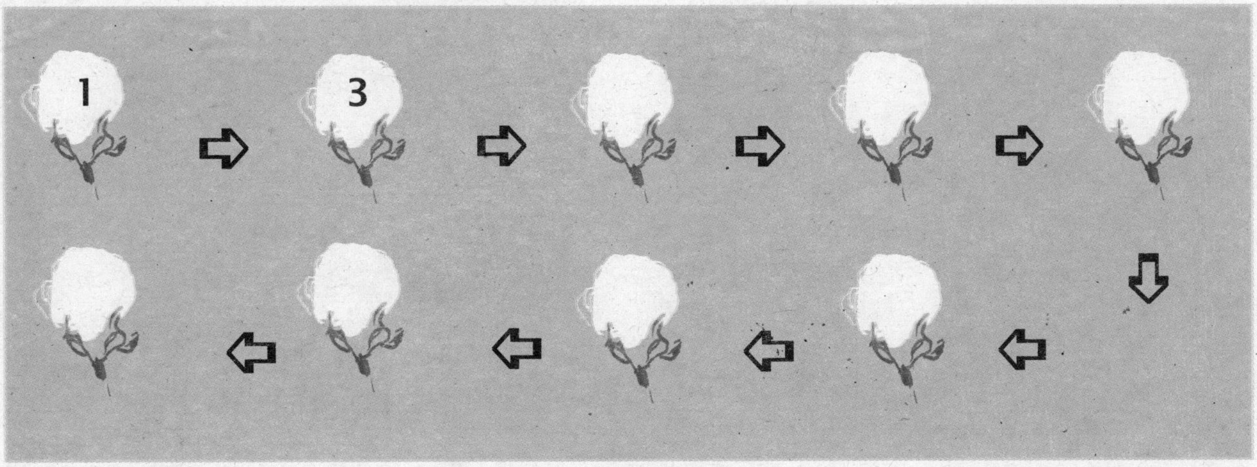

Glossary

Ginning mill: A factory where seeds are removed from cotton bolls. The cotton is pressed into bales to be sent for spinning into thread.

Exporter: A person who sells goods abroad.

Profit: The amount that is left or gained from earnings after deducting all the costs. If the costs are more than the earnings, it would lead to a loss.

CHAPTER 10

Struggles for Equality

In this book, you have read about people like Kanta, the Ansaris, Melani and Swapna. The thread that connects all of these lives is that they have been treated unequally. What do people do when they face such inequalities? History is full of examples of persons who have come together to fight against inequality and for issues of justice. Do you recall the story of Rosa Parks in Chapter 1? Do you remember the photo-essay on the women's movement in Chapter 5? In this chapter you will learn about some of the ways in which people have struggled against inequality.

As you have already read in this book, the Indian Constitution recognises all Indians as equal before the law and states that no person can be discriminated against because of their religion, sex, caste or whether they are rich or poor. All adults in India have the equal right to vote during elections and this 'power over the ballot box' has been used by people to elect or replace their representatives.

What do you think is meant by the expression 'power over the ballot box'? Discuss.

But this feeling of equality that the ballot box provides, because the vote of one person is as good as that of another, does not extend to most people's lives. As you have read, the increasing privatisation of health services and the neglect of government hospitals have made it difficult for most poor people like Kanta, Hakim Sheik and Aman to get good quality health care. These people do not have the resources to afford expensive private health services.

Similarly, the man who sells juice does not have the resources to compete with all of the major companies who sell branded drinks through expensive advertising. Swapna does not have sufficient resources to grow cotton and, so, has to take a loan from the trader to grow her crop. This forces her to sell her cotton at a lower price. Melani, like the millions of domestic workers across the country, is forced to endure the insults and hardship of working as a domestic help because she has no resources to set up something on her own. **Poverty and the lack of resources continue to be a key reason why so many people's lives in India are highly unequal.**

On the other hand, the Ansaris were discriminated against not because they did not have the resources. In fact, despite having the money to pay the required rent, they were not able to find an apartment for over a month. People were reluctant to lease them an apartment because of their religion. Similarly, the main reason that the teachers forced Omprakash Valmiki to sweep the school yard was because he was *Dalit*. You've also read that the work women do is often considered of less value than that done by the men. All of these persons are discriminated against primarily because of their social and cultural background as well as because they are women. **Discrimination on the basis of a person's religion, caste and sex is another significant factor for why people are treated unequally in India.**

In India, it is the case that the poor consist of a majority of members of Dalit, Adivasi and Muslim communities and are often women.

Often, poverty and lack of dignity and respect for certain communities and groups come together in such powerful ways that it is difficult to identify where one aspect of inequality ends and the other begins. As you have read, *Dalit*, *Adivasi* and Muslim girls drop out of school in large numbers. This is a combined outcome of poverty, social discrimination and the lack of good quality school facilities for these communities.

According to the 2001 Census data women form 48 per cent of the population, Muslims form 13 per cent of the population, Dalits form 16 per cent and Adivasis 8 per cent.

Struggles for equality

Throughout the world – in every community, village, city and town–you will find that there are some people who are known and respected because of their fight for equality. These people may have stood up against an act of discrimination that they faced or which they witnessed. Or they may be well-respected because they treat all persons with dignity and are, therefore, trusted and called upon to resolve issues in the community.

Often, some of these persons become more widely recognised because they have the support or represent large numbers of people who have united to address a particular issue of inequality. In India, there are several struggles in which people have come together to fight for issues that they believe are important. In Chapter 5, you read about the methods used by the women's movement to raise issues of equality. The Tawa Matsya Sangh in Madhya Pradesh is another example of people coming together to fight for an issue. There are many such struggles such as those among *beedi* workers, fisherfolk, agricultural

Can you think of one person in your family, community, village, town or city whom you respect because of their fight for equality and justice?

labourers, slum dwellers and each group is struggling for justice in its own way. There are also many attempts to form cooperatives or other collective ways by which people can have more control over resources.

Tawa Matsya Sangh

When dams are built or forest areas declared sanctuaries for animals, thousands of people are displaced. Whole villages are uprooted and people are forced to go and build new homes, start new lives elsewhere. Most of these people are poor. In urban areas too, *bastis* in which poor people live are often uprooted. Some of them are relocated to areas outside the city. Their work as well as their children's schooling is severely disrupted because of the distance from the outskirts of the city to these locations.

This displacement of people and communities is a problem that has become quite widespread in our

The reservoir of the Tawa river.

country. People usually come together to fight against this. There are several organisations across the country fighting for the rights of the displaced. In this chapter we will read about the Tawa Matsya Sangh – a federation of Fisherworker's cooperatives – an organisation fighting for the rights of the displaced forest dwellers of the Satpura forest in Madhya Pradesh.

Originating in the Mahadeo hills of Chindwara district, the Tawa flows through Betul, before joining the Narmada in Hoshangabad. The Tawa dam began to be built in 1958 and was completed in 1978. It submerged large areas of forest and agricultural land. The forest dwellers were left with nothing. Some of the displaced people settled around the reservoir and apart from their meagre farms found a livelihood in fishing. They earned very little.

A dam is built across a river at sites where one can collect a lot of water. This forms a reservoir and as the water collects it submerges vast areas of land. This is because the wall of the dam across the river is high and the water spreads over a large area. This is a photo of the submergence caused by the Tehri dam in Uttarakhand. The old Tehri town and 100 villages, some totally and some partially, were submerged by this dam. Nearly one lakh people were displaced.

What issue is the Tawa Matsya Sangh (TMS) fighting for?

Why did the villagers set up this organisation?

Do you think that the large-scale participation of villagers has contributed to the success of the TMS? Write two lines on why you think so.

In 1994, the government gave the rights for fishing in the Tawa reservoir to private contractors. These contractors drove the local people away and got cheap labour from outside. The contractors began to threaten the villagers, who did not want to leave, by bringing in hoodlums. The villagers stood united and decided that it was time to set up an organisation and do something to protect their rights.

The newly formed Tawa Matsya Sangh (TMS) organised rallies and a *chakka jam* (road blockade), demanding their right to continue fishing for their

livelihood. In response to their protests, the government created a committee to assess the issue. The committee recommended that fishing rights be granted to the villagers for their livelihood. In 1996, the Madhya Pradesh government decided to give to the people displaced by the Tawa dam the fishing rights for the reservoir. A five-year lease agreement was signed two months later. On January 2, 1997, people from 33 villages of Tawa started the new year with the first catch.

With the TMS taking over the fishworkers were able to increase their earnings substantially. This was because they set up the cooperative which would buy the catch from them at a fair price. The cooperative would then arrange to transport and sell this in markets where they would get a good price. They have now begun to earn three times more than they earned earlier. The TMS has also begun giving the fishworkers loans for repair and the buying of new nets. By managing to earn a higher wage as well as preserving the fish in the reservoir, the TMS has shown that when people's organisations get their rights to livelihood, they can be good managers.

Top: Members of the TMS protesting at a rally. Above: A member of the cooperative weighing the fish.

Can you think of an incident in your life in which one person or a group of people came together to change an unequal situation.

Adaptation of a song written as part of the Right to Information campaign by Vinay Mahajan:

The Right To Know

My dreams have the right to know
Why for centuries they have been breaking
Why don't they ever come true

My hands have the right to know
Why do they remain without work all along
Why do they have nothing to do

My feet have the right to know
Why from village to village they walk on their own
Why are there no signs of a bus yet

My hunger has the right to know
Why grain rots in godowns
While I don't even get a fistful of rice

My old mother has the right to know
Why are there no medicines
Needles, dispensaries or bandages

My children have the right to know
Why do they labour day and night
Why is there no school in sight

What is your favourite line in the above song?

What does the poet mean when he says, "My hunger has the right to know"?

Can you share with your class a local song or a poem on dignity that is from your area?

Creative expression against inequality

While some join protest movements to fight inequality, others might use their pen, or their voice, or their ability to dance to draw attention to issues of inequality. Writers, singers, dancers and artists have also been very active in the fight against inequality. Often, poems, songs and stories can also inspire us and make us believe strongly in an issue and influence our efforts to correct the situation.

The Indian Constitution as a living document

The foundation of all movements for justice and the inspiration for all the poetry and songs on equality is the recognition that all people are equal. As you know, the Indian Constitution recognises the equality of all persons. Movements and struggles for equality in India continuously refer to the Indian Constitution to make their point about equality and justice for all. The fishworkers in the Tawa Matsya Sangh hope that the provisions of the Constitution will become a reality through their participation in this movement. By constantly referring to the Constitution they use it as a 'living document', i.e., something that has real meaning in our lives. In a democracy, there are always communities and individuals trying to expand the idea of democracy and push for a greater recognition of equality on existing as well as new issues.

Over 1,500 persons attended a public hearing in Lucknow in 2001 to protest violence against women. Over 15 cases of violence against women were heard by a jury of eminent women who played the role of judges. This people's jury helped highlight the lack of support in the legal system for women who seek justice in such cases.

Issues of equality are central to a democracy. In this book, we have tried to highlight issues that pose a challenge to this idea of equality in a democracy. These, as you have read, include the privatisation of health services in the country, the increasing control that business houses exert on the media, the low value given to women and their work, and the low earnings made by small farmers who grow cotton. These issues substantially affect poor and marginalised communities, and therefore, concern economic and social equality in the country.

What role does the Constitution play in people's struggles for equality?

This is the core of the struggle for equality in a democracy. The dignity and self-respect of each person and their community can only be realised if they have adequate resources to support and nurture their families and if they are not discriminated against.

Can you make up a social advertisement on equality? You can do this in small groups.

References

- Dreze, Jean and Aparajita Goyal. 2003. 'Future of Mid-day Meals'. In *Economic and Political Weekly.*
- Hossein, Sakhwat Rokeya. 1905. (reprint) 1988. *Sultana's Dream.* Feminist Press, New York.
- Kumar. Krishna. 1986. "Growing Up Male" in *Seminar 318.*
- Mazumdar, Indrani. 2007. *Women and Globalization: The Impact on Women Workers in the Formal and Informal Sectors in India.* Stree, Kolkata.
- Mead, Margaret. 1928, 1973. (edition) *Growing Up In Samoa.* American Museum of Natural History, Washington D.C.
- Medical Council of India, http://www.mciindia.org/Rules-and-Regulation/Ethics%20Regulations-2002.pdf
- Parks, Rosa. 2000. *Quiet Strength.* Grand Rapids, Zondervan, Michigan.
- Rashsundari Devi. 1999. *Words to Win.* Translated and with an introduction by Tanika Sarkar. Zubaan, New Delhi.
- Roy, Tirthankar. 1999. 'Growth and Recession in Small-Scale Industry: A Study of Tamil Nadu Powerlooms' *Economic and Political Weekly.*
- Supreme Court of India, *Paschim Banga Khet Mazdoor Samity of Ors. Vs. State of West Bengal & Anr.* (Hakim Seikh case, date of judgment: 6 May 1996, http://judis.nic.in/supremecourt/imgs1.aspx?filename=15597)
- Valmiki, Omprakash. 2003. *Joothan: A Dalit's Life.* SAMYA, Kolkata.
- World Health Organization, *Essential medicines and health products*, http://www.who.int/medicines/services/inn/en/
- *www.cehat.org/rthc/policybrieffinal.pdf*
- *www.infochangeindia.org*
- Zubaan. 1996. *Poster Women: A Visual History of the Women's Movement in India.* Zubaan, New Delhi.

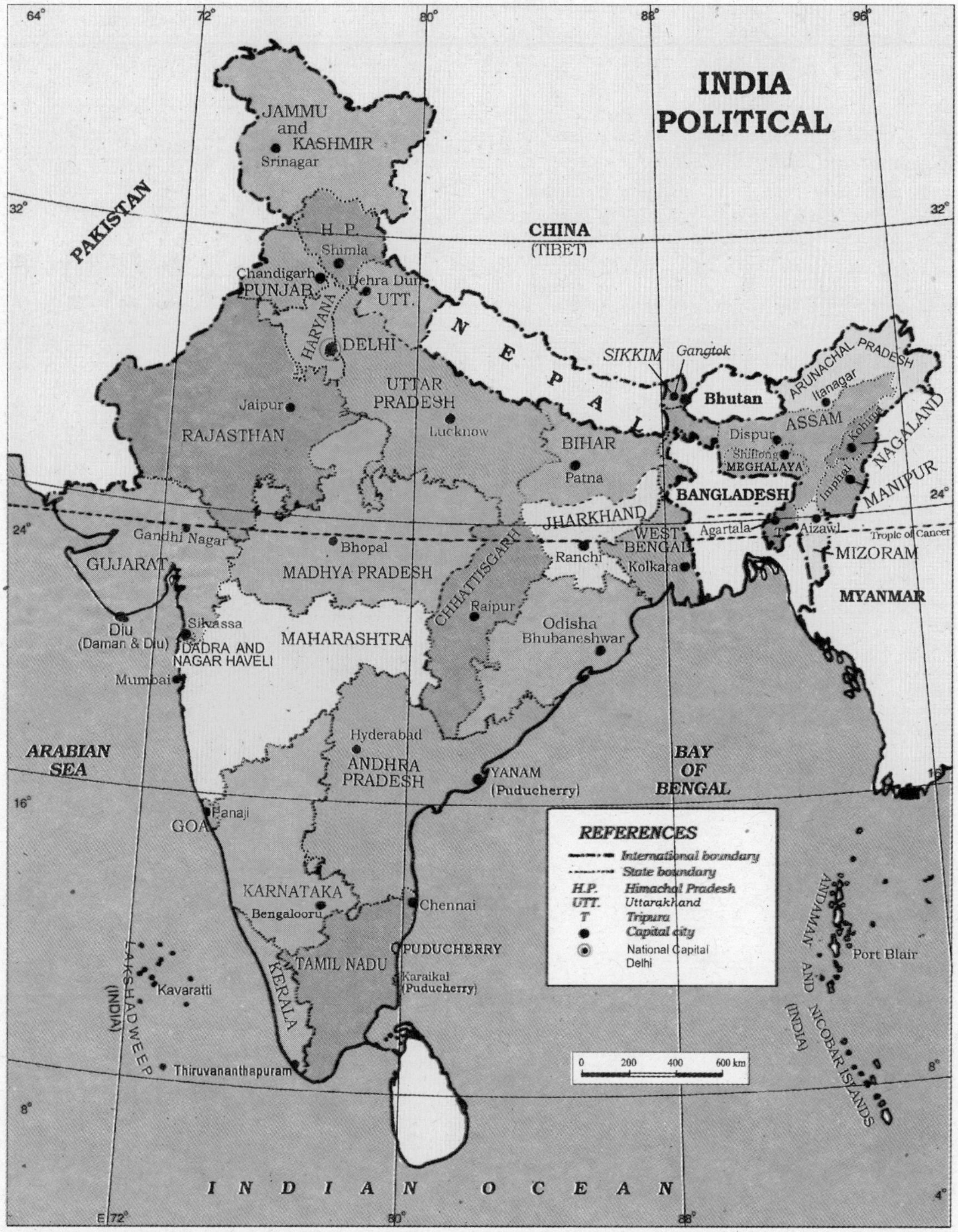

1. © Government of India, Copyright 2006
2. The responsibility for the correctness of internal details rests with the publisher.
3. The territorial waters of India extend into the sea to a distance of twelve nautical miles measured from the appropriate base line.
4. The administrative headquarters of Chandigarh, Haryana and Punjab are at Chandigarh.
5. The interstate boundaries amongst Arunachal Pradesh, Assam and Meghalaya shown on this map are as interpreted from the "North-Eastern Areas (Reorganisation) Act, 1971," but have yet to be verified.
6. The external boundaries and coastlines of India agree with the Record / Master Copy certified by Survey of India.
7. The state boundaries between Uttarakhand & Uttar Pradesh, Bihar & Jharkhand and Chhattisgarh & Madhya Pradesh have not been verified by the Governments concerned.
8. The spellings of names in this map have been taken from various sources.

** Telangana became the 29th State of India on the 2nd June 2014, after the reorganisation of the State of Andhra Pradesh.*

Notes